4.91
LGR

Paul Coleman Cochran
G.T.S.
New York
1970

THE DIACONATE NOW

THE DIACONATE NOW

EDITED BY RICHARD T. NOLAN

Edmond LaB. Cherbonnier

Theodore Parker Ferris

Edward R. Hardy

Kenneth Scott Latourette

Richard T. Nolan

George H. Emerson

Georges Florovsky

Josef Hornef

Arthur H. Legg

Robert S. Paul

Mary P. Truesdell

CORPUS BOOKS
Washington—Cleveland

Corpus Instrumentorum, Inc.
1330 Massachusetts Ave., N.W.
Washington, D.C. 20005

First Printing 1968

Copyright © 1968 by Richard T. Nolan

Library of Congress Catalog Card Number: 68-15781

PRINTED IN THE UNITED STATES OF AMERICA

PREFACE

In 1963 a bishop of the Episcopal Church laid his hands on my head and said, "Take thou authority to execute the Office of a Deacon in the Church of God committed unto thee; In the Name of the Father, and of the Son, and of the Holy Ghost. Amen." Three days later began my month's supply ministry in a parish whose rector was on vacation. Except for a Sunday supply priest, I was quite on my own for all practical purposes. As a matter of curiosity, I took up the Book of Common Prayer to see again what specific functions I had as a deacon; academic theory and ordination promises had suddenly acquired a jolting dimension of existential reality! Finding listed some tasks I felt unprepared for, and some that perhaps were not to be done, I ministered as I could for the four weeks.

When I returned to the final months of my sojourn as a master in the Choir School of the Cathedral Church of Saint John the Divine, New York, I sought to satisfy my lingering curiosity about the diaconate, a curiosity now safely academic. For myself, teaching mathematics and participating in some liturgical functions seemed quite peripheral to the order. Even my colleagues in parish work seemed to lack a specifically diaconal ministry, instead being sort of junior clergy due for an ecclesiastical and pecuniary raise in six months to a year. I wondered whether the Sacred Order of Deacons had become outmoded?

Neither persons nor books I sought out furnished unanimity on the tasks for the contemporary deacon. Thus, with the encouragement from some senior clergy, I set out to gather essays about the diaconate from some perceptive Christians. As I wrote to one of the contributors, "the study will contain varying points of view, inasmuch as the Christian traditions value the diaconate with much variety. Our purpose is to air some of the more significant issues and to offer these thoughts to the Church. It is not our purpose to achieve unanimity, but rather a common spirit of scholarly reflection."

The first chapter is concerned with the development of the diaconate, followed by surveys of its uses and, as authors have wished to comment, potentials in Protestantism, Roman Catholicism, Orthodoxy, Anglicanism, and the Church of South India.

A word about the chapter on Anglicanism is in order. The diaconate in this Communion is practiced with diversity. This comprehensive feature led the editor to seek expositions on these practices with the hope that from a "practical" point of view, certain representative uses of an ordained diaconate could be explored.

No treatment of this ministry would be complete without a word about deaconesses. Concluding the study is a chapter speculating on the role of the diaconate in the Church's future. If the thoughts on these pages offer the Church a better understanding of its diaconal heritage and potentials, the study will have served its purpose.

I wish to express my appreciation and gratitude to the contributors, who entrusted their written words to a novice editor. My thanks go, also, to the several persons who offered suggestions as the project developed. In particular, I am grateful to the Rev. Lee A. Belford, Ph.D., Chairman and Professor of Religious Education at New York University, who permitted me to undertake the initial phases of this task within an independent study course, and who offered helpful criticisms. Thanks go, also, to the Rev. Ian D. K. Siggins, Ph.D., Assistant Professor of Church History, Yale University, who directed me to Corpus Books. Special mention must be made of the meticulous care with which Miss Carol Steiman, Secretary of the Religion Department, Trinity College (Ct.), typed the manuscript; she went far "beyond the call of duty" in attending to details. The drudgery of checking the galley proofs was shared with my mother, who checked the manuscript with me, and my father, who accepted graciously our occasional neglect during my visit at their Fort Lauderdale home; my appreciation of their willingness to assist cannot go unmentioned. Finally, I should like to express sincere gratitude to the Rev. Harold C. Gardiner, S.J., for his guidance during the final phases of the project's completion. For the completed work, however, I accept full responsibility.

RICHARD T. NOLAN

Bristol, Connecticut, 1967

CONTENTS

the Orthodox Church, with special emphasis on the deacon's liturgical functions.

Richard T. Nolan introduces this chapter with a survey of the order of deacons in Anglicanism. Subsequently, Dr. Theodore Parker Ferris focuses upon an "internship" use of the office, and Archdeacon George H. Emerson discusses his involvements as a "perpetual deacon." Concluding this chapter, Dr. Edmond LaB. Cherbonnier offers his thoughts as one who has chosen to remain in deacon's orders.

by Arnold H. Legg

Since that Church is a sort of synthesis of Anglican, Methodist, Presbyterian, and Congregational traditions, Bishop Legg examines the theory and practice of the Church of South India regarding the diaconate. Its attitudes toward that office are particularly instructive.

by Mary P. Truesdell

The exact place of the office of deaconess in modern ecclesiastical economy has not been fully resolved. Its history and potentials are offered by Deaconess Truesdell.

by Kenneth Scott Latourette

Dr. Latourette takes a church historian's view of the future of the diaconate.

EDWARD R. HARDY

DEACONS IN HISTORY AND PRACTICE

I

The episcopate is indeed the essential ministry of the Catholic Church, since the apostolic office includes all forms of ministry, and from it all specialized forms can be produced. But as the very terms used indicate, the diaconate can be considered as the basic form of ministering within which all others are specializations. Our English translations obscure the frequency of the terms *diakonos* and *diakonia*, and cognate verbs, in the New Testament. Jesus is indeed the "Apostle and high priest of our profession" (Heb 3,1), but the "diaconate of Christ"[1] is more conspicuously emphasized in the Gospels, perhaps just because it needs emphasis. He came, not to be deaconed to, but to diaconize; and so He requires that whoever wishes to be greatest among His followers should be their *diakonos* (Mk 10,43-45 and parallels)—a principle sacramentally symbolized today by the fact that (normally, at least) no man becomes a bishop unless he has first been ordained to the diaconate. *Diakonia* is the general term in the New Testament for service or ministry. The noun or cognate verb can therefore be used of the ministry of angels (Mk 1,13; Heb 1,14), of apostles (Acts 1,17; 2 Cor 3,6; 6,4), or of helpful souls generally, such as Peter's wife's

11

mother (Mk 1,31), the women who followed the Lord (Lk 8,3), and the recipients of Hebrews (Heb 6,10). The term is indeed of such general application that it can be said that just as Christ has His *diakonoi*, so Satan has his (2 Cor 11,15), though the immediate reference here seems to be to false apostles who were no true *diakonoi* of Christ. *Diakonia* can be used for the work of the Gospel in general, for which the saints are to be perfected (2 Cor 3,7-9; Eph 4,12). But on the other hand, the ministry of service can be distinguished from other vocations more conspicuous, but no more honorable, such as prophesying, presiding, teaching, or working miracles (Rom 12,7; 1 Pt 4,11). Indeed, the most specific use of *diakonia* is for ministry to physical needs, such as the gifts sent to the saints at Jerusalem (2 Cor 8,4; 9,1), where the church was responsible for daily *diakonia* to its widows (Acts 6,1).

The New Testament still leaves us uncertain when *diakonos* and *diakonia* began to refer to a specific order, as well as to a function, which might be either general or specific. St. Paul exercised the *diakonia* of the apostleship (Rom 11,13); but what was that of Archippus at Colossae? (Col 4,17). A later generation would probably have called him bishop of, or at least a bishop at, Colossae; yet we are told that Onesimus might, in his place, have diakonized to Paul (Phil 13). Much as *apostolos* may refer to the apostles of Christ or the messengers of the churches, so one may be a *diakonos* of Christ, or of God, or exercise *diakonia* to the brethren, or to one's superior, such as an apostle (see Acts 19,22, where Timothy and Erastus diakonize to Paul). The few pagan uses of *diakonos* seem to refer to the assistant or acolyte to a priest; Lucian's satirical biography of the false prophet, Alexander of Abounoteichos, tells us that he received his training while serving as helper and *diakonos* to an older thaumaturge. [2]

Terms sometimes used interchangeably with *diakonos* are *doulos* and *hyperetes*. The former refers primarily to slavery and the latter emphasizes subordination, which doubtless explains why *diakonos* alone survived as a technical term. But the

New Testament usage of all three is similar. Paul describes himself regularly as slave of Christ (whose service is perfect freedom); and the term is later used of James (Jas 1,1) and Peter (2 Pt 1,1). Epaphras is also a *doulos* of Christ, and he and Tychicus are fellow-servants (*syndouloi*) of Paul, but *diakonoi* rather than *douloi* of the congregation (Col 1,7; 4,7, 12). *Hyperetes* can be used in general senses; Luke, however, employs it more specifically of the *shammas* in the synagogue at Nazareth (Lk 4,20), and of the vocation of St. Paul, who himself employs it of the apostolic ministry (Acts 26, 16; 1 Cor 4,1; see Lk 1,2). The cognate verb is used of the help given to St. Paul by his friends at Caesarea (Acts 24,23), which is suggestive of the duties of later deacons in relieving confessors in prison. Finally, John Mark was *hyperetes* to Paul and Barnabas (Acts 13,5), later apparently succeeding Tychicus as *diakonos* to Paul (2 Tim 4,11).

The description of the mysterious Phoebe as a *diakonos* (not *diakonissa*) of the church at Cenchreae and patroness of the apostle and many others (Rom 16,1-3) is perhaps semitechnical. Presumably she was a wealthy Christian distinguished for her *diakonia*, like Chrysostom's friend and supporter at Constantinople, the deaconess Demetrias, three centuries later. Nearby at Corinth itself the household of Stephanas, the firstfruits of Achaea, had devoted themselves to *diakonia* to the saints and deserved to be obeyed (1 Cor 16,15-16); this would seem to be an application of the principle that he who is chiefest should be servant of all. Stephanas was apparently as close to a bishop as the church at Corinth would tolerate—were the members of his household, then, *diakonoi*, and if not, why not?[3] One may see here an anticipation of the presence of deacons as secretaries and attendants in episcopal households—as can be illustrated in the will which Gregory of Nazianzus drew up when he was bishop of Constantinople,[4] and is met with in the Eastern Orthodox Church today.

Some influence in the fixing of terminology (one cannot say how much) was exercised by the Septuagint of Is 60,17, which refers to the officers of the people of Israel as *episkopoi* and *diakonoi*. In writing to Philippi, St. Paul addresses the saints of that city "with bishops and deacons" (Phil 1,1); one must remain uncertain whether this refers to two definite orders, or simply to those who guided and served the church, which might indeed mean the same individuals in different capacities. The titles recur in the local ministry contemplated in the *Didache*—"elect for yourselves *episkopoi* and *diakonoi* worthy of the Lord" (*Didache* 15)— but the meaning as well as the time and place of that evidence is uncertain. We reach more solid ground when Clement of Rome, writing in that city about A.D. 100, tells us that the apostles established bishops and deacons in the various churches (I Clement 42). Fortunately, the disorders at Corinth affected only the former order, so Clement has little to tell us of the latter. But he seems to be the first to suggest a parallel between the deacons of the church and the levites of the Old Testament (and, indeed by implication, with the non-commissioned officers of the Roman army) in accordance with his feeling for hierarchy (*ibid.*, 37, 39). Conditions in the province of Asia a few years earlier are probably reflected in 1 Timothy. While its usage of bishop and presbyter is uncertain, its directions for deacons are crystal-clear: they are to be respectable married citizens, sound in the faith, and if they diaconize well (the term has now definitely become technical), will gain "a good standing" (translation in the Revised Standard Version). This does indeed seem to offer them the prospect of promotion to a higher order (1 Tim 3,8-13).

No use has been made in this discussion of the sixth chapter of Acts, since that passage is more important as a precedent for the later diaconate than as a source of information about the New Testament *diakonia*. It does, however, tell us that the Seven were chosen for the *diakonia* of tables (or perhaps banks, which the word can also mean?) so that the Twelve might concentrate on the *diakonia* of the Word. Actually, the only two we hear of again, Stephen and Philip, function as evangelists rather than as deacons—perhaps a precedent for some modern developments of the Anglican diaconate—but the picture suggested in Acts 6 is followed in the relation of bishops and deacons from the second century to the sixth.

II

The golden age of the diaconate as a distinct order is the patristic period from A.D. 100 to 600, from Ignatius of Antioch to Gregory the Great. The bishop, as the normal pastor and priest of the local church in each city, needed assistance in his various functions, liturgical, administrative, and pastoral; and the order of deacons was ready to undertake this duty. Presbyters fell relatively into the background until, with the division of dioceses into parishes (in the modern sense), the parish priest became the *pastor loci*, taking over most of the day-to-day sacerdotal functions of the bishop and the *diakonia* of the deacon. That, however, was still in the future. In St. Ignatius' pictures of normal church structure the bishop is not so much successor of the apostles as vicar of God; the deacons are related to him as Christ to the Father, and the poor presbyters can be compared only to the council of the apostles (e.g., Trallians 3). Usually, however, Ignatius merely mentions deacons as part of the threefold hierarchy—but with a reminiscence of St. Paul's usage, he singles them out as his fellow-servants (*syndouloi*), of Christ, presumably (Philadelphians 3; Smyrnaeans 12)—and there is a hint of one of their later functions in the suggestion that a deacon would be the natural messenger to send to a distant church (from Philadelphia to Antioch; Philadelphians 10). Some thirty years later Justin Martyr shows us the "serving of tables" developing into a liturgical function, when "those whom we call deacons" distribute "the food which is called Eucharist" both to the congregation present and those absent (1 Apology, 65-67). Indeed, Ignatius seems already to have thought of the duties of the deacons at the Eucharist as the center of their office; the "deacons of the mysteries of Jesus Christ . . . are not *diakonoi* of food and drink, but *hyperetai* of the church of God; they must therefore guard themselves from reproach as from fire" (Trallians 2).

The Church Orders give us our best picture of the functioning of the third-century diaconate. One of these documents even suggests that a very small church might be ministered to by a bishop and deacon with no presbyters,[5] but the Ignatian picture is the usual one. Writing at Rome about 200, Hippolytus tells us that the deacons brought up the oblations at the Eucharist and assisted at baptism, where two held the holy oils for the presbyter and a third entered the water with the candidates. They should assemble daily to receive the bishop's instructions, and with their assistants, the subdeacons, were responsible for reporting illness to the bishop so that he might visit the sick. In the prayer for their ordination the bishop would ask:

> grant the Holy Spirit of grace and care and diligence to this thy servant, whom thou hast chosen to minister to thy church and to bring up in holiness to thy sanctuary that which is offered to thee by thine appointed high priests, so that ministering without blame and in a pure heart, he may by thy good will be found worthy of this exalted office. . . .
> (*Apostolic Tradition*, 9)

Hippolytus first shows the anxiety to keep deacons in their place which becomes conspicuous in the next century—perhaps because his running fight with Callistus began when they were respectively presbyter and deacon. The distinctions he makes became permanent; deacons are not ordained to the priesthood, but to serve the bishop—hence they do not join in the council of the clergy with the presbyters, and are ordained by the bishop alone without the laying-on of the hands of the presbyter.[6] Hippolytus indeed allows them to administer the eucharistic cup only if there are not enough presbyters present; on the other hand, their clerical status does allow them to bless the bread at the *agape* (*Apostolic Tradition* 23, 26, 30, 33).

No such suspicion of diaconal presumption appears in the *Didascalia Apostolorum,* coming from some Syrian church about the middle of the century, for its author, the bishop, symbolizes the Father, the deacon the Son, and the deaconess the Holy Spirit—he evidently thought in Syriac in which the word "Spirit" is feminine.[7] The deaconess' duties are limited to personal ministry to women; the deacon must be ready for whatever the bishop directs. He may receive the contributions of the faithful, though passing them on at once to the bishop, and should minister devotedly to the sick and infirm, if necessary laying down his life for the brethren. If this phrase is more than rhetoric, it would refer to dangers incurred in time of pestilence or persecution.[8] In church one deacon stood by the oblations and another at the door as a kind of usher; at some point before the prayers a deacon proclaimed, "Is there anyone who has aught against his fellow?"[9] The *Didascalia* directs that there should be deacons in proportion to the size of the congregation. Rome, however, had by this time restricted the number to seven, in imitation of Acts 6; a letter of Pope Cornelius (251-53) lists the clergy of the Catholic Church (of Rome)—"one bishop, 46 presbyters, seven deacons, seven subdeacons," and numerous minor clerics.[10]

The deacons' duty to attend the bishop bound them together even at moments of crisis. So at Carthage Cyprian's deacons stepped forward to stand beside him at his martyrdom on Sept. 14, 258, and 45 years later the deacons of Cirta shamefacedly joined their bishop in his apostasy.[11] The persecution of Valerian was planned, primarily, as an attack on the property of the church, so it is not surprising that it began with the arrest of the Bishop of Rome and four of his deacons as they were officiating in the catacombs, and their martyrdom on Aug. 6, 258. Four days later the deacon Laurentius followed his colleagues; and there is no reason to doubt the story that, in the interval, he laid up in heaven the treasures of the church by distributing them to the poor, for whose benefit he had administered them in time of peace. Known to us as St. Lawrence, he became the first object of widespread popular veneration among the martyrs of the Roman Church, doubtless, in part, because his functions as principal deacon had made him well-known. The services for St. Lawrence's day are one of the oldest parts of the Roman liturgy; one of the antiphons puts in his mouth words that express the proper relation of an ancient deacon to his bishop in life and death—"Where do you go without your son, O Father? where, O holy priest, are you going without your minister?"[12]

Much of our knowledge of fourth-century and later deacons comes from the canons of councils, which were more concerned to prescribe what they should not do than to describe their normal functions. In 314 the Council of Arles (canon 16) firmly said that they should not presume to offer the Eucharist as had happened in many places, presumably during the confusion caused by the recent persecution.[13] It has indeed been suggested that under the Ignatian rule a safe Eucharist is one celebrated by the bishop or his deputy (Smyrnaeans 8); it could indeed be that in this period a deacon, as well as a presbyter, might represent the bishop at the altar.[14] But in the liturgy the deacon had his own separate and important function; and Hippolytus was as clear as any later Catholic writer that presbyters are ordained to the priesthood and deacons are not. The Council of Nicaea assumes the same principle in its canon 18, which carries a step further the principle laid down at Arles; deacons must not administer the Eucharist to presbyters, since those who have no right to offer ought not to give the Body of Christ to those who do. Deacons, the council defines, are "ministers (*hyperetai*) of the bishop and inferiors of the presbyters," and so should receive in due order from the bishop or presbyters, and not presume to sit among the latter. The picture envisaged is that of the crown of presbyters in the *synthronos* on either side of the bishop's seat in the apse. Some time around the mid-century, the Council of Laodicea adds that a deacon should not sit in the presence of a presbyter unless he invites him to—but may expect due honor from subdeacons and other lesser clergy. What is forbidden to the latter indicates some of the rights of deacons: they enter the sacristy (*diaconicon*), and handle the sacred vessels; they wear the stole (*orarion*), here first mentioned as a badge of rank; and are allowed to "give the bread and bless the cup," which probably means to preside at the *agape* (canons 20-22, 25).

Deacons are naturally included in general regulations for the higher clergy, such as those forbidding them to enter taverns (Laodicea, canon 24), a constant preoccupation of ancient and mediaeval councils, and those endeavoring to keep them in their original dioceses (e.g., Nicaea, canons 15 and 16). Their financial duties may lead us to suppose that canons forbidding the clergy to receive usury (Nicaea, canon 17), or to serve as business managers or agents (Chalcedon, canon 3), or as conductors or procurators, that is, administrators of imperial estates (African Code 16), were specially aimed at deacons. On the other hand, deacons were likely to be designated as the clerical stewards (*oikonomoi*) which the Council of Chalcedon required each bishop to appoint (canons 25 and 26). By the middle of the fifth century, it was assumed that the higher clergy would not marry after ordination (Chalcedon, canon 14)—even early in the fourth century the Council of Ancyra had allowed deacons to marry only if they had declared their intention in advance (canon 10). By 400 the Latin Church was already disposed to require continence of deacons and their superiors (African Code 3 and 4, from a Council of Carthage about 390).

At Rome, especially, the deacons stood out as conspicuous figures, since they were limited to the sacred number of seven, and were more closely connected with the pope than were the more numerous presbyters. About 370 an anonymous writer attacked their presumption in a treatise significantly entitled "On the Boastfulness of the Roman Deacons" (*De Iactantia Romanorum Levitarum*).[15] No matter how important they were in practice, deacons must remember that presbyters outranked them; after all, one ordained a deacon presbyter, and not vice versa. If, at Rome, deacons recommended candidates for the presbyterate and then presented them to the bishop (a duty which the Roman Pontifical and English Prayer Book still ascribe to the archdeacon), they were acting on behalf of the congregation of the faithful (see Acts 6,5-6). But, the author adds, deacons did rank ahead of all except priests (i.e., bishops and presbyters—*exceptis enim sacerdotibus, quibus obsequium debent, omnibus praeponuntur diaconi*). Jerome who, as a presbyter, was ready to defend the status of his order against both the others, became aware of this discussion and sums it up in one of his cutting epigrams:

> What can ail the servant of tables and widows that he gives himself airs as the superior of those at whose prayers the body and blood of Christ are produced? [*ad quorum preces corpus Christi sanguisque conficitur* (Letter 146)].

The importance of the Roman deacons led to their wearing the dalmatic, which, in this period, was the semi-formal dress of the Roman senator. Granted as a privilege to some others, this usage spread in the course of the Middle Ages to deacons of the Western Church generally, replacing, even in church, their proper costume, the simple chasuble which the deacon removed and threw over his shoulder during his active liturgical duties. In the vestigial form of the folded chasuble (*planeta plicata*) replaced during the Mass by a strip of material called the "broad stole," the older dress survived in the Roman ceremonial until eliminated in recent liturgical reforms.[16]

The formal liturgical duties of the deacon, in later times the most conspicuous aspect of the office, developed out of his work as server of tables and as usher. Already at the end of the late fourth century, Theodore of Mopsuestia calls him the "herald of the church." In this capacity he is the most active participant in the Eastern Orthodox liturgy, proclaiming the biddings for prayer to which the choir responds *Kyrie eleison*, and directing the congregation with exclamations such as "Let us attend" and "The doors, the doors," the latter at the moment when, formerly, his assistants closed the doors after the departure of the catechumens.[17]   He remained responible for bringing the oblations to the altar; and the reading of the Gospel, formerly like other lessons entrusted to readers, came to be given to the deacon as a suitable mark of honor. At Rome, deacons acted also as cantors for the elaborate Gradual between Epistle and Gospel, until Gregory the Great transferred this function to singers, since it was leading to the choice of candidates for the diaconate based, mainly, on musical ability. In the Roman rite the deacon still prepares the chalice and joins with the celebrant in offering it; and, as long as communion in both species survived, he had, in spite of Hippolytus' feelings on the subject, a special connection with the administration of the chalice.[18]   This survives in a solemn papal Mass where the deacon, though now actually a cardinal deacon in episcopal orders, brings the chalice to the pope for his communion, and it has been revived in modern Anglican practice.

When there were a number of deacons, a special importance attached to the bishop's personal assistant; he came to be called the archdeacon—the title properly means "bishop's deacon," rather than "chief of the deacons." He would often be, for practical purposes, the second most important person in the diocese, and a likely candidate for the episcopate. From such a position at Alexandria Athanasius succeeded Bishop Alexander in 328, and Dioscorus succeeded Cyril in 444. To make an archdeacon merely one of the presbyters was, in effect, a degradation under the form of a promotion. In 453 Leo the Great reprimanded Anatolius of Constantinople for thus mistreating his Archdeacon Aëtius; and in 591/592 Gregory the Great intervened on behalf of Archdeacon Honoratus of Salona against his bishop, Natalis, who "attempted, it is said, craftily to degrade the aforesaid archdeacon, under color of promoting him to a higher dignity."[19]

The cardinal deacons of Rome, as we may begin to call them, were suitable representatives of their chief at the imperial court. In this capacity the deacon, Pelagius, enjoyed the friendship of the Emperor Justinian; on behalf of Pope Vigilius he sat in the court of the Patriarchs which met at Gaza (about 540) to depose their colleague, Paul of Alexandria,[20] and when Vigilius was summoned to Constantinople in 546, Pelagius returned to the war-torn city "with great wealth" for its relief, presumably from the Sicilian estates of the Roman Church. He was, in effect, the pope's vicar; as such he stood on the steps of St. Peter's with the Scriptures in his hands to meet the Gothic King Totila, and, as occasion required, interceded for the people of Rome with King and Emperor.[21] In his Byzantine exile Vigilius was accompanied by at least a subdeacon,[22] and when he died on his way home in 554 Pelagius was his logical successor. A similar career is that of Gregory the Great, who, 30 years later, was called from his monastery on the Aventine and made *septimus diaconus*, which I presume means junior cardinal deacon. As such he represented Pope Pelagius II at Constantinople (as his *apokrisiarios*, in Latin *responsalis*), and then returned to Rome as abbot of St. Andrew's until called to the episcopate himself in 590. He then sent one of his deacons to Constantinople, and functions that would be considered diaconal were exercised by the stewards of the papal estates such as Peter, "subdeacon of Campania," to whom many of his letters are addressed.[23]

III

The canons of the so-called Quinisext Council, which met at Constantinople in 691-692 to supplement the Fifth and Sixth Ecumenical Councils with a canonical code, record the rules governing the diaconate in the Eastern Church as they have since remained. Deacons might not marry after ordination as subdeacon, but if already married, could continue to live with their wives, in contrast with the rule of the Roman Church that already demanded celibacy or, at least, continence. But the rule "husband of one wife" was interpreted to exclude those who had married widows, as well as those married twice after baptism (canons 3, 6, 13). Even a deacon who holds a high office is not to take his place before a presbyter, unless he is acting as a representative of his patriarch or metropolitan (canon 7). The proper age for ordination to the diaconate is fixed at 25; and the general custom of having as many as needed is defended against that of limiting the number to seven. The Fathers of the Council agreed with John Chrysostom, as do many modern scholars, that the Seven of Acts 6 were not deacons in the later sense of the term (canons 14, 16). Rome still preserved the other tradition, which had the support of one of the fourth-century Eastern councils (Neocaesarea, canon 15).

Even at Rome there were, doubtless, by this time others in deacon's orders besides the seven cardinals. The latter had, in the seventh century, an important place in the administration of the papal city. In each of the seven ecclesiastical regions which had replaced the fourteen civil regions of imperial Rome, the center of what we would call social services was a *diaconia* with its church, storehouses, hostel, and bathhouse, run by monks under the supervision of the region.[24] This was the last expression of the diaconate in its ancient form; the general tendency of the period separated the functions of *diaconia* from necessary connection with the office of deacon. One aspect, perhaps a cause, of this development is the rise of a parallel hierarchy inside the increasingly important monastic world. St. Benedict, for instance, assumes that his monastery will need deacons as well as priests for its services, the abbot sending up suitable candidates for ordination if the need is not met by novices already in orders (*Rule*, chapters 60, 62). Under the abbot as ruler and pastor, however, functions which could be considered diaconal were performed by such officials as the cellarer (chapter 32). Eastern monasteries still do not consider ordination the regular goal of the monastic career, although they have priests and deacons among their members; but by the ninth century, Western monks, as well as the clergy of episcopal churches, normally proceeded to the priesthood after some years in a mainly liturgical diaconate—an example is the career of the Venerable Bede, who was ordained deacon at the early age of nineteen, and priest at the canonical age of thirty (*Ecclesiastical History*, V, 24). About 840 the abbey of St. Denis had among its 123 monks one bishop, thirty-three priests, seventeen deacons, twenty-four subdeacons, and seven acolytes.[25]

Though the mediaeval diaconate retained its status as a major order, it was thought of, mainly, in terms of its formal liturgical functions. As with the priesthood, attention in the ordination service shifted from the imposition of hands and the prayer to more impressive, but actually less significant, moments, such as the vesting in a dalmatic and the tradition of the book of Gospels, considered as the instrument of the deacon's most conspicuous public function. To this ceremony pontificals attached the words, "Take thou authority to read the Gospel as well for the living as the dead," that is, in ordinary as well as requiem Masses.[26] By a fairly old tradition, the newly ordained deacon (or one of them if there were a number) at once exercises his office by reading or singing the Gospel, while the Eastern Orthodox ordination follows a reverse procedure, the candidate standing in his place as subdeacon until admitted to the diaconate just before his communion.

Later mediaeval deacons seem either to have been candidates for the priesthood, or else to have been such as wished to be attached to the ecclesiastical world without assuming the responsibilities of the priestly office. The archdeacon became a kind of ecclesiastical justice of the peace, the legal representative of the bishop, and the later history of his office belongs to Canon Law rather than to the diaconate as such—although, in 1102, an English council, out of a general sense of the fitness of things, ordered that archdeacons should be deacons (Council of Westminster, canon 4). The office could be held also by a canon lawyer in major or minor orders, or even used merely as a source of revenue while the duties were delegated—hence the question raised, semi-seriously, by theological students, "Can an archdeacon be saved?" To this Thomas Aquinas replied charitably that archdeacons, like parish priests, have a certain spiritual greatness, since on account of their zeal they undertake the cure of souls. They likewise give proofs of stability, for they remain firm and constant in the midst of dangers. They are, further, upright in their intention, and just in their dealings. Why then should we deny that they are in a state of perfection? (*On the Religious State*, Chapter 21).

But Thomas feels obliged to answer in the negative, since, unlike monks, archdeacons do not take vows. At the time, a typical example of the worldly archdeacon seemed to be young Thomas of London, Archdeacon of Canterbury under Archbishop Theobald. When he transferred his talents to the royal service as chancellor to Henry II, he scandalized the world by his gay clothes and his addiction to chess, which was then played as a frivolous game and had a reputation rather like that of poker today. Only on the day before his consecration to the episcopate (on Trinity Sunday, 1162) did Becket put worldly things behind him at his ordination to the priesthood—which, incidentally, illustrates that the older custom of consecrating deacons directly to the episcopate, *per saltum*, had now died out, partly because it had come to be generally held that the priesthood was the highest of the sacred orders and the episcopate merely a special form of it.

It is an example of the conservatism often found in the Roman Church that its cardinal deacons (and in a few cases like that of Hildebrand, cardinal subdeacons) continued to serve as papal legates and administrators without proceeding to the higher order until called to an office which required it. So they might, as deacons, preside over bishops and archbishops in council. A cardinal deacon might well be the logical candidate for the papacy; in one such case, when Cardinal Lothair became Pope Innocent III in 1198, he administered the affairs of the Church for several weeks as a deacon before proceeding to his ordination and consecration.[27]   In the confused state of church order in the late Middle Ages and Renaissance, prolonged diaconates might be found among the worldly, the respectable, or the devout; though celibacy was assumed, deacons were sometimes dispensed from it on renouncing the ecclesiastical state. One extreme is represented by Caesar Borgia who was cardinal deacon and Archbishop of Valencia (i.e., technically archbishop-elect and administrator, happily for the see, *in absentia*) until he abandoned this status in the hope of founding a dynasty; the other, by Reginald Pole, who was made a cardinal deacon when in exile from the England of Henry VIII, and who was still a deacon when he served as one of the three presidents of the Council of Trent in 1545-47. He was briefly (though not very seriously) considered as a possible husband for his cousin, Mary Tudor, and, like Becket, was ordained to the priesthood only on the eve of his consecration to the episcopate. Respectability is represented by Pius II's nephew, Cardinal Piccolomini, who administered the see of Sienna for forty years as a deacon until elected to the papal chair in 1503; or the Hapsburg Cardinal, Archduke Albert, who served his cousin, Philip II, as general and viceroy, and was allowed to abandon his orders to marry Philip's daughter, Isabella, when sent to govern the Spanish Netherlands in 1598. An English parallel is the career of William Warham, who remained a subdeacon while serving Henry VII as a diplomat, and then in his early fifties was rapidly promoted to higher orders, and advanced to the primatial see in 1502/1504.

IV

The Reformers, quite naturally, saw no great similarity between the ceremonial or political diaconate of the sixteenth century and that which they found in the New Testament. A typical statement is that of the Church Order proposed for Hesse in 1526: dalmatics are no longer to be used, since

> no one in the future should wear the vestments of popish deacons or subdeacons, since we do not wish to give support to those orders which were introduced without the testimony of the divine oracles. For Scripture knows no other ministers

than bishops, presbyters, and deacons of the poor. We do not find a single iota about mass-priests or deacons in either Testament, though the assistants of the bishops may not improperly be called *diaconi*, that is, ministers; for deacon means minister and *diaconia* ministry.

The same document later provides for these two kinds of deacons: assistant ministers to bishops, whom it does not distinguish from presbyters, and deacons of the poor.[28] From the latter usage derives the diaconate as known in the Reformed Churches; among Lutherans the term has been, and sometimes still is, used in the sense of an assistant minister as, for instance, in the year of diaconate that some American Lutherans plan for their theological students before the final year of the seminary course.

The English Reformation first expressed itself on the diaconate in the *Necessary Doctrine and Erudition* of 1543, commonly called the King's Book. In treating of the sacrament of Orders it follows the scholastic line in being vague about the difference between priests and bishops. On deacons it quotes Acts 6 and I Timothy 3, and then adds that

> their office in the primitive church was partly in ministering meat and drink and other necessaries to poor people found of the church, partly also in ministering to the bishops and priests, and in doing their duty in the church. And of these two orders only, that is to say priests and deacons, scripture maketh express mention, and how they were conferred of the apostles by prayer and imposition of their hands.[29]

The medieval system continued, however, through the Henrician period, with few, if any, ordained to the diaconate except those who intended to advance to the priesthood. The establishment of the monastic churches, which were refounded as secular cathedrals in several cases, included a deacon and subdeacon, but this seems merely to mean minor canons who would be prepared to serve as readers of the Gospel and Epistle at High Mass.

The modern Anglican understanding of the diaconate begins with the first English Ordinal of 1550 in which Cranmer, whom we may presume to have been its compiler, returns to the older idea of three sacred orders, bishops, priests, and deacons. He added to the solemnity of ordination to the two latter by introducing the formal examination that the Pontifical had provided only for the consecration of bishops. In this he defines the duties of a deacon as follows:

> It perteyneth to the office of a Deacon in the Churche where he shalbe appoynted to assiste the Prieste in deuine seruice, and speciallye when he ministreth the holye Communion, and to helpe him in distribucion thereof, and to instructe the youth in the Cathechisme, to Baptise and to preache yf he be admitted therto by the Bisshop. And furthermore, it is his office where prouision is so made to search for the sicke, poore and impotente people of the parishe, and to intimate theyr estates, names, and places where thei dwel to the Curate, that by his exhortacion they maye been reliued by the parishes or other conueniente almose: wil you do this gladly and wyllingly?

Perhaps absent-mindedly, he left the diaconate without any formal ordination prayer except for one after the litany at the beginning of the service (since 1662 used as the Collect). This defect has been repaired in some, though not all, of the modern revisions of the Prayer Book. Cranmer's definition of the office follows generally the lines laid down in 1543; as in other parts of his liturgical reform, he aims to work back to the ancient institution as he understood it, while preserving continuity with the existing one. The diaconate envisaged in 1550 would have been a different order from the priesthood, rather than merely a step towards it; in effect, it enlarged the duties of the parish clerk into those of a parochial assistant. Had this possibility been actualized, it might have made some of our modern developments unnecessary, but the Ordinal recognized that, actually, most candidates for the diaconate would also aim at the priesthood. The Preface fixes the minimum age for deacons at 21 and priests at 24; the final prayer asks that they "may so wel use themselues in thys inferior offyce, that they may be found worthi to be called unto the higher ministeries in the Church." Taken literally, this seems to pray that they may become bishops, and the final rubric warns the new deacon that he must continue in that office

the space of a whole yeere at the least (excepte for reasonable causes, it bee otherwyse seen to his ordenarie) to thentent he may be perfecte, and wel experte in the thinges apperteyning to the Ecclesiasticall administration . . .

before being advanced to the priesthood—which seems to accept the idea of the diaconate as a final stage in theological education. Instead of the Book of Gospels alone, the Anglican deacon was (and is) given the New Testament; and with it he is commissioned, not only to read the Gospel, like his medieval predecessor, but to preach it if so licensed. Actually, Latin Canon Law already contemplated this possibility, as it still does —in the fourteenth-century Gerard de Groot, the founder of the New Devotion, had accepted ordination to the diaconate in order that his previous activity as a lay preacher might be regularized (see *Codex Juris Canonici,* 1917, canon 1342, 1). Whatever may have been Cranmer's ideas about the diaconate, they remain among the unfulfilled projects of the English Reformation. The practical question before the Elizabethan Church in this connection was whether it would introduce the Reformed diaconate, or be content with a reform of the mediaeval diaconate not much more radical than that being undertaken in the Roman communion under the guidance of the Council of Trent. The latter prevailed, but not without some controversy. The exiled congregations of Queen Mary's reign appointed ministers and deacons on the Reformed model, and at least one of Elizabeth's bishops seems to have visualized this as the ideal. In 1562 James Pilkington of Durham wrote that, under the Gospel, there is no need of popish flummery, but only of "a pulpit, a preacher to the people, a deacon for the poor, a table for the communion, with bare walls, or else written with scriptures."[30] Elizabethan phraseology often uses "minister" for "priest," as, when in 1578, the Genevan Dean of Durham, William Whittingham, was forced to admit "that he is neither deacon nor minister according to the order and law of this realm."[31] But, in effect, the Elizabethan bishops continued to ordain deacons and priests as their predecessors had done— though sometimes, especially in the early years of the reign, admitting a candidate to both orders at one service. This extreme shortening of the diaconate to a half-hour or so seems to have been due to the urgent need of filling gaps in the ministry after 1559, and later sometimes to the feeling of some Puritans that episcopal ordination was merely a legal formality. From their point of view the complaint was justified that the Church of England had no true diaconate; as it was put in the *Admonition to Parliament* in 1571:

> Touching deacons, though their names be remaining, yet is the office finally perverted and turned upside down; for their duty in the primitive Church was to gather the alms diligently and to distribute it faithfully; also for the sick and impotent persons to provide painfully, having ever a diligent care that the charity of godly men were not wasted upon loiterers and idle vagabonds. Now it is the first step to the ministry, nay rather a mere order of priesthood.

To this John Whitgift and, after him, Richard Hooker replied that ancient deacons had assisted the presbyters in church as well as ministering to the poor, and that the examples of Stephen and Philip were enough to justify the extension of their commission to preaching and baptizing, which Puritans had criticized on the ground that "the deaconship must not be confounded with the ministry."[32] But this left the question unanswered whether there was a special vocation of the diaconate for which the Anglican reform had not provided.

Canonically, Anglican rules for the diaconate remain

much as the Elizabethans left them. In the *Constitutions and Canons* of 1603, canon 32 is headed "None to be made Deacon and Minister both in one Day"; it, rather unhistorically, describes the diaconate as "a step or degree to the Ministry" —deacons need not necessarily serve for a whole year, but at least till another Embertide, so that "there may ever be some trial of their behaviour in the office of Deacon, before they be admitted to the order of Priesthood." In 1662 the Prayer Book restricted baptism by deacons to the absence of the priest, and raised the minimum age for the ordinand to twenty-three "unless he have a Faculty," i.e., dispensation, which has, in fact, rarely been granted. Even the shortening of the diaconate to less than a year, which both Prayer Book and Canons contemplate, seems never to be allowed under normal circumstances. The extreme case did occur in 1661 when those of the Scottish ministers chosen for the episcopate who had not received episcopal ordination were made deacon and priest in one day.

In the eighteenth century, colonial candidates who could not spend a year in England were often advanced rapidly: Samuel Johnson, for instance, was ordained on March 22 and 31 in 1723; Samuel Seabury on December 21 and 23 some 30 years later. William White, on the other hand, received a Faculty for ordination to the diaconate on Dec. 23, 1770, some months before his 23rd birthday, but waited for his priesthood till April 25, 1772.[33] Any normal English clerical career since the Restoration will show the canonical one-year diaconate: John Keble, for instance, born in 1792, was ordained deacon in 1815, and priest in 1816; John Henry Newman, similarly, in 1824 and 1825. A less famous cleric, the diarist, James Woodfoorde, born in 1740, thus describes his ordination to the diaconate on May 29, 1763:

> At nine o'clock this morning went to Christ Church with Hooke, and Pitters, to be ordained Deacon there by Hume Bishop of Oxford. There were 25 ordained Deacons and 13 Priests. We all received the Sacrament. . . . We were in C.

Church Cathedral from nine o'clock this morning till after twelve. For wine this afternoon in the B.C.R. paid 0.0.6.[34]

Except for the last entry this would be typical of general ordinations in English cathedrals in the eighteenth or nineteenth centuries; they are somewhat shorter now. Prolonged, or indeed permanent, diaconates sometimes occurred in academic circles; two famous cases are those of the learned Martin Routh who was ordained deacon in 1777, became President of Magdalen College, Oxford, in 1791, and was advanced to the priesthood when he undertook also the charge of a parish in 1810;[35] and Charles Lutwidge Dodgson, better known as Lewis Carroll, who, during his long service as Student (i.e., Fellow) of Christ Church, Oxford, never advanced beyond the diaconate which he received in 1861.

The canonical rules of the Episcopal Church in the United States are naturally derived from those of the Church of England. Its first bishops sometimes ordained men rapidly to meet the needs of the moment. Thus Seabury advanced some of his first deacons to the priesthood almost immediately, and in 1795 made the future Bishop Griswold deacon in June and priest in October. But since their first adoption in 1789, the Canons have considered a year's diaconate as normal; they have varied from time to time as to whether the period may be shortened, and, if so, to what extent and by what authority. Since 1907 the bishop and his standing committee must concur in the arrangement, and the minimum period is six months (except that since 1961 Canon 35 allows a four-month diaconate for candidates who have served in the ministries of other Churches). The American Canons and Prayer Book have returned to the older minimum age of twenty-one for deacons, thus sometimes requiring a two- or three-year diaconate (e.g., W. A. Muhlenberg, ordained in 1817 and 1820); and since 1832 a "title" (as it is called in England), that is, assurance of a proper clerical position, is required only at ordination to the priesthood, and not necessarily for the diaconate.[36]

V

It remains to add a few notes about the historic diaconate as found in various parts of the Church today. In the Eastern Orthodox Church the parish clergy are often ordained to the priesthood after a day or two in the diaconate—the order of Orthodox ordination services in which priests are ordained at the Offertory and deacons at the Communion prevents the extreme shortening to one service. But the Greek Orthodox are close to some aspects of the ancient diaconate, since the celibate clergy often remain deacons while serving under the bishop in non-parochial ministries. An example within the present writer's experience was that of Leontios Leontiou, afterwards Archbishop of Cyprus, who was a deacon and diocesan preacher in Paphos (studying at the General Theological Seminary in New York) when elected Bishop of Paphos in 1930. In the Russian Church, on the other hand, outside monasteries the permanent diaconate is mainly a liturgical and musical office; and I understand that in the Syrian, Coptic, and Ethiopian Churches boys are made deacons much as in the West they might be made acolytes.

Since the Council of Trent the Roman Catholic Church has taken the diaconate seriously; but in practice it is conferred only on candidates for the priesthood, usually in their last year at the seminary. In Montreal, Cardinal Paul-Emile Léger arranged to have his seminarians spend their last vacation as parish assistants, gaining pastoral experience while discharging those functions which canon law allows to deacons, such as preaching, baptizing, and taking Communion to the sick. A form of the permanent diaconate, now extinct, survived till 1870 among clerics who found their careers in the papal diplomatic service or the administration of the papal states. Famous examples are Jules Mazarin (1602-61), who passed from the papal diplomatic service to the French, and rose to become cardinal and chief minister of France during the minority of Louis XIV; Cardinal Ercole Consalvi (1757-1824), who ably represented Pius VII in the negotiations for the Napoleonic Concordat in 1801, and at the Congress of Vienna; and Pius IX's Secretary of State, Cardinal Giacomo Antonelli (1806-76). With the end of the papal states in 1870, there was no longer any need for these secular cardinals, and the last of them died early in the pontificate of Leo XIII—although until 1960 the Roman missal contained directions for the funeral mass of a cardinal deacon who had not been advanced to the presbyterate.[37] Cardinal deacons (no longer limited to seven) are now always at least presbyters, and indeed John XXIII directed that in the future all cardinals should be consecrated to the episcopate.

In the Church of England the diaconate seems now invariably to be considered as the final year of preparation for the priesthood. However, the order of Readers has gradually been allowed to undertake all the functions which Cranmer contemplated for the diaconate, except for public baptism, but including, by special permission, the administration of the chalice.[38] It could be said that the readers, who in England are not called lay readers, are in effect the diaconate of the English Church. In the United States the Episcopal Church has for more than a century considered the possibility of a permanent diaconate. In the discussions which followed the Muhlenberg Memorial of 1853, the diaconate was considered mainly as an order of evangelists, which was not the primary character of the ancient diaconate.[39] This may explain why the provision for candidacy for the diaconate only, which was introduced into the Canons in 1871, was dropped in 1904. As someone commented, the main characteristic of permanent deacons seemed to be their impermanence, that is, their tendency to aspire to the priesthood. It is still possible to be ordained to the diaconate without taking the full canonical examinations required for priest's orders; and in 1952, provision was again made for the ordination as deacon of a man desirous of serving in that office "without relinquishing [his] secular occupation and with no intention of seeking advancement to the priesthood" (canon 34, section 10, as of 1964). The diaconate is here conceived of in terms of voluntary pastoral and liturgical assistance. There are now some 200 of these "permanent deacons," and they do seem to serve a useful purpose, especially since the laity in General Convention had three times defeated the proposal to follow England in licensing lay readers to administer the chalice.[40] Formally these permanent deacons differ from others only in that they are not included in the operations of the Church Pension Fund (and are perhaps not licensed to preach, which other deacons seem to be automatically); and they are not forbidden to change their minds and qualify for the priesthood after all. But their existence does give some recognition to the principle that the diaconate is a distinct order and not merely a step towards the priesthood. In one diocese (Long Island), a permanent deacon (the Rev. John H. Mears) has occupied the position of diocesan treasurer, which the ancient church would have considered a proper function of the diaconate.

Every deacon is in fact a perpetual deacon, and if ordained to the priesthood or episcopate continues to exercise the functions of the diaconate; in fact he may spend much of his time in duties which the early Church would have considered diaconal. For many centuries the Church has abandoned the ancient custom of ordination *per saltum* (though they have occurred in some recent reunion plans), and so, under all normal circumstances, every man ordained to the priesthood has first been made a deacon. As presbyter or bishop he should continue to stir up in his life the grace of the diaconate, that is, the gift of service in union with the serving Christ. As of old, the Lord Jesus says to us, "Where I am, there shall my *diakonos* be" (Jn 12,26); and the spirit of the order, whether held alone or in conjunction with others, is beautifully expressed in the prayer offered by an Orthodox bishop when he admits a man to it:

> O God our Saviour, who by thine incorruptible voice didst appoint unto thine Apostles the law of the diaconate, and didst manifest the first Martyr, Stephen, to be of the same; and didst proclaim him the first who should exercise the office

of a Deacon, as it is written in thy Holy Gospel: Whosoever desireth to be first among you, let him be your servant: Do thou, O Master of all men, fill also this thy servant, whom thou hast graciously permitted to enter upon the ministry of a Deacon, with all faith and love, and power, and holiness, through the inspiration of thy holy and life-giving Spirit; for not through the laying-on of hands, but through the visitation of thy rich bounties, is grace bestowed upon thy worthy ones; that he, being devoid of all sin, may stand blameless before thee in the terrible day of thy judgment, and receive the unfailing reward of thy promise:

For thou art our God, and unto thee do we ascribe glory, to the Father and to the Son and to the Holy Spirit, now and ever and unto ages of ages. Amen.[41]

ROBERT S. PAUL

THE DEACON
IN PROTESTANTISM

I. THE PRIMACY OF THE CHURCH

In the year 1571 a Separatist congregation in London petitioned
against the ill-treatment they had received at the hands of the
English episcopal authorities. They complained that the queen's
officers had imprisoned and killed "the Lord's servants, as our
minister, Richard Fitz, Thomas Bowland, deacon, one [named]
Partridge and Gyles Fowler." We know little enough about
Thomas Bowland, the deacon, except that some years earlier he
had been the leader of a Separatist congregation meeting at the
Plumbers' Hall, and that together with Randall Partridge and
some others he had been examined by Archbishop Grindall
in June, 1567. He then re-appears as the deacon of Richard
Fitz's gathered church, and seems to have died as a result of his
imprisonment for nonconformity.[1]

Perhaps in this instance his career as a Separatist is of less
importance to us than the fact that he was specifically designated
"deacon," for it illustrates the carefully defined church order by
which Separatists and Puritans sought to re-constitute the
Church according to the New Testament. It is sometimes too
easily assumed that the dispute between the Elizabethan bishops
and the Puritan wing of the Church concentrated upon minor

matters of liturgical practice, whereas a study of such documents
as the petition cited above reveals that its true center was the
nature of the Church. As the authors of the Puritans' *First
Admonition to Parliament* declared, "Neither is the controversy
betwixt them [the bishops] and us (as they would bear the
world in hand) for a cap, a tippet or a surplice, but for great
matters concerning a true ministry and regiment [i.e., ruling]
of the church according to the word. . . ."[2] As far as this wing
of Protestantism is concerned, any discussion of particular "orders" within the Church must start from the doctrine of the
Church itself.

Herein lies our problem for, although there appears to be
agreement among Protestants generally about the nature of the
Church, there is less agreement about its form, and we cannot
assume that there is a uniform approach to ecclesiology. In
several Protestant denominations the pattern of parochial church
life, and even the duties and titles of the officers appointed, do
not differ very widely, but could it be said that Baptists, Congregationalists, Disciples, and Presbyterians hold identical doctrines of the Church, or that their view of "deacons," for
example, is the same?

Obviously not, and yet when we look at these denominations together, or with the Methodists and Lutherans, among
whom the pattern of church life may be somewhat different,
we recognize that there is a root which is common to the whole
of Protestantism, and which is bound to affect all its variant
ecclesiologies.

This common ground is, I suggest, the principle that we
are justified by faith in Jesus Christ, and that our authority for
this claim is to be found primarily in the Bible. Both the principle of justification by faith and the biblical authority on which
it is based are equally important for Protestant doctrines of the
Church, for in the scriptural record justification is related at
every point to the community of faith. If we take the doctrine
seriously, we must take the Church seriously. What is the pattern that should be taken by a Church founded on faith in

Jesus Christ? Is it laid down in the Scriptures or in the Church's own tradition? Or is it to be decided according to the needs of each generation?

Differences of interpretation were almost bound to enter. At first the Reformers seem to have expected Christian rulers to answer the basic question for them, but as the relationship between Church and State became increasingly suspect, it became more and more clear that the churches could not so easily get rid of the question. Protestantism was forced to address itself to a definition of the Church, but within that question it discovered others: what is the will of Christ regarding the structure of the Church; what is the relation of the congregation to its ministers and to the sacraments; who are the Church's proper officers; what is the nature of its authority under the Holy Spirit?

Beneath the many answers that have been given to these questions, and which have contributed to the complexity of Protestantism, we can, perhaps, discern two main approaches to the doctrine of the Church. There have been those who, in emphasizing the primacy of justification by faith, have tended to regard the doctrine of the Church as secondary. They have not been particularly concerned to discover or defend a form of polity for the Church from Scripture, but have regarded such questions as essentially pragmatic. Insofar as the Church's structure does not deny any Gospel principle, the Church may adapt its form to suit the needs of its mission in any age.

Denominations such as Lutheranism and Methodism have shared this basic attitude, but it is also an attitude that cuts across the denominational lines, for there have been those like the Anglican Archbishop, Richard Bancroft, or the Congregationalist, Robert Dale, who, while holding a preference for one or another polity, have believed that there is no one form of church order that has been laid down as of divine right.[3] At its best, those who represent this position emphasize that the Church is to be the servant of the Gospel it proclaims, and that it must be subject to the rule of the Spirit. At its worst, this view of the Church can degenerate into a mundane kind of pragmatism that denies the presence of the Holy Spirit, and reduces the Church to a wholly human society.

On the other hand, there are those who have insisted that a God-given form of the Church is to be found in Scripture. Whether they are Anabaptists arguing with Luther and Zwingli in the sixteenth century, Presbyterians and Congregationalists arguing with each other in the Westminster Assembly, or Disciples arguing with everyone else on the American frontier, they all have insisted that God has set down the form of the Church in the New Testament. If one relieves the term "high church" of its purely liturgical connotations, these are the high churchmen of Protestantism. Against the claims of pope or bishops for a form of the Church *ex jure divino* based on historical continuity, they have claimed a form that is *ex jure divino* based on Scripture. At their best, they have uncompromisingly maintained the God-given nature of the Church as essential to the divine plan of salvation, but at their worst they have been guilty of stifling the Holy Spirit in the most rigid forms of literalism. In seeking to restore a New Testament pattern of the Church it is possible to deny the Spirit that gave life to the Church of the New Testament.

All this is prolegomena to our subject, but it is necessary prolegomena. It is not the purpose of this essay to pass judgment on the relative merits of these basic attitudes to the doctrine of the Church, but simply to indicate the context within which any discussion of orders within Protestantism must take place. The office of deacon in the church structure of any Protestant denomination must be seen as part of the whole debate on the nature of the Church, for it is only as an aspect of that doctrine that Protestants would regard it as relevant.

II. THE OFFICE OF DEACON

It is generally true that Protestantism knows no order of deacons as a distinct grade in a clerical hierarchy. In those denominations that have not been dominated by the desire to restore the New Testament Church, the office of deacon may not appear at all, or its appearance will be governed by geographical, national, or cultural considerations—the desire to maintain continuity with the past, political necessity, or practical efficiency. Accordingly, although there may be some pressure in the Swedish context for Lutheranism to revert to the threefold conception of the ministry, the office of deacon is not known in Lutheranism generally. The same would be true of Methodism. The office of deacon is not used in the Methodist Church of Britain where Methodism was born, for John Wesley appears to have reached the conclusion that in the early Church the presbyter and the bishop were of essentially the same order,[4] and the system he established included the elements of several forms of polity.

But it must be remembered that Wesley did not intend to break from the Church of England, and perhaps the system he bequeathed to British Methodism is to be seen less as his blueprint for a new denomination than as supplementing the orders of the established Church. If this is so, then we may reasonably argue that American Methodism was true to the spirit of Wesley when it introduced the threefold structure of orders into its own system. Within the situation as it was in America at the end of the eighteenth century, Methodism could not rely on the ministrations of Anglican clergy.

But precisely for this reason Methodism does not contribute directly to our understanding of what Protestants mean by deacons. In its American form, Methodist orders seem to be but a pale imitation of the Anglican model—imitation because deacons occupy relatively the same place as Anglican deacons in the scale of clerical authority, and pale because Methodists would insist that they do not represent a distinct *order* of ministry. For all practical purposes, a deacon in the Methodist Church in America is an ordained person on his way to becoming a fully qualified and recognized minister, and he is, to that extent, on probation. He is able to perform some of the duties of the eldership, but he has no distinct duties or authority which are not also possessed by the Elder.

A discussion of the office of deacon in Lutheranism and Methodism is likely to be somewhat thin, but I would submit that a discussion of the diaconate, in its wider sense, would not be. If our basic concern is with *diakonia*—ministry and service within the Church—then one would have to look to the many forms of lay service in the history of Methodism, to the leaders of its class meetings, and to the circuit stewards who, without the actual name deacon, have expressed the actual calling and service of the New Testament deacon.

This is the kind of diaconate that Luther recognized. He declared that:

> . . . the diaconate is a ministry, not for reading the Gospel or the Epistle, as the practice is nowadays, but for distributing the wealth of the Church among the poor, that the priests may be relieved of the burden of temporal things, and may give themselves more freely to prayer and to the word. It was for this purpose, as we read in the Acts of the Apostles, that deacons were appointed.[5]

This life of practical service is maintained in the Lutheran deacons and deaconesses of the Inner Mission in Europe,[6] or in the nursing deaconesses known in America. The work of deacons may be unknown in large parts of Protestantism, but the work of *diakonia* is not, for it is of the essential nature of the Church itself.

The application of this concept of service to the work of deacons in the Church will be seen as we turn to those churches that have sought to restore a New Testament pattern of churchmanship. Indeed, the place of the deacon in any Protestant denomination depends very largely on the extent to which the denomination has held, and in practice continues to hold, a "restorationist" view of the Church.

In the churches that have tried to restore the New Testament Church in form as well as in faith, we are at once presented with a clearer and yet more complex picture of the deacon. Historically, the aim in each case was to restore the New Testament office with its New Testament functions, but in the course of history other factors have entered to modify and change this original intention, so that denominations that began by asserting very similar things may now find themselves far apart.

In the fourth book of Calvin's *Institutes* the Reformer shows that a very clearly articulated doctrine of the Church is integral to his system, and he makes clear also that his authority is the pattern of the Church in the New Testament. This scriptural appeal may be illustrated among Calvin's modern followers by citing the recent report on *The Nature of the Ministry* presented to the 176th General Assembly of the United Presbyterian Church in the U.S.A. It states that "The scriptures clearly point out Deacons as distinct officers in the church, whose business it is to take care of the poor, and to distribute among them the collections which may be raised for their use." It then adds a note which may come from more modern times: "To them also may be properly committed the management of the temporal affairs of the church."[7]

Luther appeals to the same Scripture in almost exactly similar terms, but he did not seek to set up a church structure on this basis.[8] It is this reliance on the Bible for the *form* of the Church, and to justify the place and function of its officers in the modern world, that distinguishes the Church of Calvin from that of the Lutheran reformation which had preceded it; and, insofar as those who reacted to Calvin did so on the basis of the New Testament, there was bound to be more in common in the actual pattern of church polity between Calvin and the radicals who opposed him than there was between Calvin's form of the Church and Luther's. Since all restorationist views of the Church were ultimately based upon the same scriptural references, there were bound to be many features of church life and practice that were common to them all. In seventeenth-century England it was not difficult for Presbyterians, Congregationalists, and Baptists to agree that the proper officers for a Christian congregation were the pastor (whom they regarded as the presiding elder or bishop of New Testament times), the teaching elder, the ruling elder, and the deacon.

The scriptural functions of the deacon (as described in the Presbyterian statement above) were regarded as so clear and obvious that some of the early statements are extremely reticent about his duties;[9] they were all to be found delineated in the Book of the Acts. All these early statements, however, seem to have drawn a clear line between the various forms of eldership and the deacons. They represented distinct and separate orders. Presbyterian Puritans and Congregational Puritans might argue whether elders who had been ordained to a particular congregation could exercise jurisdiction in other congregations, but they were agreed on the officers that the local church must appoint, and that there was a distinction to be made between elders and deacons. There is a passage in *An Apologeticall Narration* of 1644 where the Congregational authors insist that they owned a polity that was in all essentials the same as that of other Reformed Churches, and they declared: "For officers and public rulers in the church, we set up no other but the very same which the reformed Churches judge necessary, and as instituted by Christ and his apostles, that is, Pastors, Teachers, Ruling Elders (with us not lay but ecclesiastic persons separated to that service), and Deacons."[10] The distinction is between the various forms of eldership and deacons.

In Congregationalism this distinction seems to have lessened during the seventeenth century as the structure became simplified and possibly as the hold on synodical authority became weaker among the Churches. Comparatively early, the office of the teaching elder became vested in the work of the pastor, and the special functions of the ruling elder disappeared, so that deacons were drawn into a more prominent position in the congregation. Although the *Savoy Declaration* of 1658 still mentions teachers and elders with the pastor as ordained officers of the congregation, it goes on to say: "And of a Deacon, that he be chosen by the like suffrage [of church members], and set apart by prayer, and the like Imposition of Hands."[11] It is clear from the emphasis in the rest of the document that deacons are not regarded as of the same order as pastors, teachers and elders, but it is equally obvious that in stressing that they were chosen and commissioned by a "like" method, they were in some sense regarded as sharing in the ministry of the Church.

In the local congregation today Presbyterians and Reformed Congregationalists, Baptists, and Disciples share very similar church organization that reflects their historic appeal to the New Testament norm, namely, an ordained ministry (which, in the case of Presbyterian and Reformed churches, continues to include elders as well as pastors) and a lay diaconate elected by the congregation.

In practice this sometimes means that the board of deacons is little more than a committee elected to administer the material affairs of the parish, and although Congregationalist and Baptist deacons are open to the same criticism, perhaps the danger of the office losing its spiritual basis is more obvious where the eldership retains control of the spiritual life of the congregation.

To the extent that Congregationalists and Baptists have been concerned to maintain the spiritual and ecclesial character of the diaconate, they have tried to achieve it by frankly uniting within it the duties formerly undertaken by ruling elders. The British Baptist, the late H. Wheeler Robinson, describes the local deacons as usually "an Executive Committee, with a good deal of variety in the powers assigned to them, so that in practice they often become a sort of 'Kirk-Session'. . . . The deacons combine, however, the spiritual functions of the 'eldership' with the financial functions of the diaconate in the Presbyterian Church."[12] Similarly, a recent Congregational statement from America says that "Deacons are men who are elected to assist the pastor in helping the church to envision and achieve its spiritual possibilities,"[13] and, although their traditional functions are not omitted, it is significant that the writer directs the deaconesses to the specific task of administering the congregation's charitable concern: they are "women who are elected by the church to render spiritual and social service to the homes of the parish members in cooperation with the deacons."[14] The same concern to stress a pastoral role for deacons is seen in a parallel statement from England. "The task to which a deacon is called," declares the author, "is to manage and direct the affairs of the Church, both temporal and spiritual," but he continues:

> a deacon's task is not primarily administrative, the stewardship of Church funds, the care of the buildings, the material side of the Church's organization. In a practical age there is a danger that this side of the work is over-emphasized and even regarded as the first and only task of a deacon. . . . The first concern of a deacon is the spiritual life of the Church.[15]

Among Disciples we can see the same concern. W. B. Blakemore, the Disciples' scholar, writing of his own church tradition, has said, "Both the Stoneites and the Campbellites, within their congregationalist polity, had a tradition of a three-fold order of the ministry. The orders comprised deacons, elders, and evangelists or pastors. Originally these were understood as the three *ministerial* offices of the local congregation," but he goes on to comment:

> . . . later generations have fallen away from this understanding, and now, despite their insistence on the priesthood of all believers which should disallow any distinctions between "clergy and laity," they think of their deacons and elders as "lay" officers, and only the pastorate is thought of as a "ministerial" office. To all intents and purposes, the Christian Churches (Disciples of Christ) stand for a single *order* of the ministry. . . . What has happened is that a former ministerial work of the eldership has been virtually lost to memory. This ministerial work of the eldership was originally a responsible participation in a spiritual concern for the spiritual welfare of the congregation. All of this concern has now devolved onto "the minister," and it is a rare elder who understands himself as sharing a general ministry of spiritual oversight.[16]

Doubtless there are differences between the Disciples' po-

sition and the views of the churches that came out of the seventeenth-century Puritan struggle, but the same pattern of churchmanship is there. However, what is significant in this passage
is not only the trend which Dr. Blakemore discerns, but also his
own criticism of it. What Congregationalists and Baptists have
been trying to recover by combining some of the pastoral functions of eldership in the diaconate, Dr. Blakemore is trying to
recover by the more healthy method of recalling Disciples' elders
to their own proper function in the Church.

It is clear that the role of lay officers, and particularly of
the deacon, has been changing in the Free Churches. What has
been happening to Congregational and Baptist deacons is nor-
mative, and is becoming very clear. In some ways the New
Testament responsibility for administering the Church's compassion has become secondary, and the deacon's principal duties
seem to be far nearer to positions which we know in the
business world—financial advisor, executive committeeman,
member of the board and the like. Perhaps as a kind of compensation we have found it necessary to stress his spiritual responsibility and even to invest him with pastoral functions that he
formerly did not have.

One can understand the reasons that have prompted this,
but I question whether it is sound theologically to confuse the
deacon's office with those of the pastoral eldership. To put it
bluntly, it may be just as erroneous and inadequate to turn the
deacon into a deputy-assistant-minister as it is to reduce him
to the position of financial advisor or member of the governing
board, and I fear this is the risk we run when we speak of him
being elected "to assist the minister in helping the church to
envision and achieve its spiritual possibilities."

Let me approach the point in another way. In Puritan
thought the diaconate represented a distinct office in the
Church, separated from the pastoral offices and to be held by
laymen. Of course, we can find plenty of evidence that the
Puritans were not modern democrats, and yet we can adduce
far more evidence that they did not intend to set up a hierarchy

in the Church. The offices of the Church were not to be thought of as ascending grades in a scale of ecclesiastical status and authority, but distinct offices because they had been ordained as such by our Lord. We may question their interpretation of the New Testament, but that was their understanding of it. Often the pastoral office was extolled and honored far beyond its deserving, but essentially the various offices in the Church were distinct, and owned specific functions that had been God-given. In this sense, a deacon was not to be thought of as an ecclesiastical non-commissioned officer midway between the officers and the ranks. He, too, had his commission which was just as solemn and imperative for him as it was for any minister. The high regard that the Puritans had for all churchly orders is illustrated in the words of Jeremiah Burroughes, one of the Dissenting Brethren in the Westminster Assembly, when he declared that "once a man be chosen as an officer in the Church, all that power that ever any in that office had since Christ's time, in any Church in all the christian world, or ever can have to the coming of Christ againe, falls upon him."[17] This would be as true for the deacon as it would be for any elder.

I suggest that the Puritans had a valuable theological insight when they insisted that the deacon represented a distinct order in the Church, and that he should be a *layman*. For he was to be a layman, chosen and commissioned with a care equal to that exercised in the recognition and ordination of a minister; the deacon would both serve the Church and work within the world. Moreover, he was a man through whose leadership in the congregation the Church's *diakonia* was to be expressed, her ministry of compassion to the world. Perhaps the most significant way forward ecclesiologically in the Free Churches would be to recognize the implications of that basic insight today.

III. DEACONS AND DIAKONIA

Several factors combine to make a reappraisal of orders in the Church an urgent priority. The new ecumenical possibilities that have arisen since Vatican Council II, the interest in the laity as the People of God, biblical theology, and the sociological critique of the Church, all invite us to undertake a deeper and more searching examination of the Church's ministry.[18] Within such a study the role and purpose of the diaconate not only have a proper place, but could very well become the point on which the whole meaning of ministry turns.

The time is favorable for such a re-study. The course of biblical and historical studies over the past half-century has proved that the ways in which we debated the nature of the Church in the past are unsatisfactory. They may bolster up our prejudices, but they do nothing to solve the ecumenical dilemma the Church faces. Whether we base our authority on literal appeals to the Church's tradition or to literal appeals to the text of Scripture, we have converted few and solved nothing, and one feels on the basis of the biblical evidence that Canon B. H. Streeter's oft-quoted but generally ignored comment is the only acceptable one: "in the words of *Alice in Wonderland*, 'Everyone has won, and all shall have prizes.' "[19] Or in the words of W. B. Blakemore, "what is needed is a conception that transcends all three of these historic doctrines of church polity, and points toward another kind of understanding which may serve a more ecumenical purpose."[20]

Perhaps the new basis, not for debate about church polities but for ecumenical dialogue about the doctrine of the Church, is to be found in biblical theology—an appeal, not to the letter of Scripture, nor to the letter of the Church's canons, but to the nature of God's redemptive work revealed in the Bible, and given to the Church as its ministry in the world. We are beginning to understand that what all wish to see in the Church is not the reproduction of a particular form of government, Catholic or Protestant, nor even to see established, in our own century, the Church structure of the first century, but rather a form and a ministry that can express the presence of the living Christ. We recognize that institutional forms, polity, ministry, cannot be ignored if we are to take the redemptive incarna-

tion of our Lord seriously, but we insist that these must reflect
and express the same Holy Spirit which directed the apostles and
helped them to establish in the world of the first century the
kind of worshipping and witnessing Church that they did. And
therefore we are not concerned any longer with proving to ourselves, or to others, that this or that office has New Testament
warrant, but with asking what particular *need* produced that
office in the Church and caused it to take the form it did. To
use the example of the diaconate, certainly deacons were appointed in New Testament times, but what were the particular
needs that brought the office into being? What were the special
duties that they undertook with regard to the Church's worship,
its social concern, and its evangelical outreach? Are we primarily concerned with maintaining an order of Christians called
deacons, or are we concerned that the Church of the twentieth
century should have within it those who can express these
aspects of her life and mission?

Of course, we are concerned here with a reappraisal of
the whole doctrine of the Church, and not simply with any one
order within it. But I suggest that at the heart of this reappraisal there must be a serious attempt to explore, for our own
day, the meaning of *diakonia* (ministry, service) as that which
defines the nature of the Church's distinctive ministry. Indeed,
it may be of some significance to note that at least one recent
Anglican writer traces the beginning of the Church's settled ministry, not to the apostles, but to the appointment of the first
deacons.[21] What is the relationship of *diakonia* in the New Testament to the New Testament deacons?

The New Testament scholars must help us; but in our
understanding of *diakonia*, for our own day, I suggest that the
history of deacons and the diaconate in Protestant churches presents us with several important insights.

1. The heart of the deacon's work for the Church is in
diakonia, and to the extent that this represents the ministry of
service, it is of the essence of all ministry in the Church. For
this reason, if for no other, the ministry of deacons cannot be

essentially different from other ministries in the Church. I have
suggested elsewhere that Protestants must regard all ministries
in the Church as dependent upon the ministry *of the Church*,
i.e., all the forms of particular ministry are dependent upon that
corporate ministry of reconciliation which the Church, as a
ministering community, receives from its Lord, and which reflects his redemptive ministry among men.[22] If *diakonia* is the
expression of this, then the ministry of deacons cannot be funda-
mentally different from any other form of ministry in the
Church, because all ministry must reflect the essential character
of the Church's corporate ministry to the world. In this sense
I believe that what Dr. W. B. Blakemore said of the early
Disciples in America was equally true of all Protestants who
have approached the doctrine of the Church *via* restorationism
—they have held to a threefold concept of the ministry in which
the deacon has his proper place.

2. On the other hand, I am less happy with the suggestion
that a line should not be drawn between clergy and laity, because I think it reflects a misunderstanding of the proper place
that each has within the life of the Church. I would hold that,
in making a distinction between an ordained eldership and lay
deacons, Puritans reached a basic insight about the nature of
the Church, and we entirely miss the point if we think of their
distinction in terms of a higher or lower status. The important
point to consider is that, although deacons were chosen with as
much care as elders, and given a similar kind of ecclesiastical
recognition, *they were not ordained*. Their leadership in the
Church was fully acknowledged, but it was acknowledged as
being exercised in a deliberately lay capacity, not, I suggest, as
a concession, nor yet as an inferior grade in a clerical hierarchy,
but as a deliberate matter of church order.

This point is of particular importance if *diakonia*, ministry,
is a calling in which the whole Church is involved, and not
merely the function of the few, for what could point more significantly to that *corporate* vocation than a distinct order of lay
representatives incorporated into the Church's official ministry

and called by that name? Therefore, I would maintain that the distinction between ordained elders and lay deacons, far from indicating clericalism, ought to be an expression of the dignity of the lay vocation, and should point directly to the ministry of the whole People of God.

3. Taking their stand firmly on the duties given to the deacon in the New Testament, the Puritans emphasized two functions as belonging distinctively to the diaconate. Deacons were required to serve tables, i.e., to distribute the elements to the people at the celebration of the Lord's Supper, and they were responsible also for dispensing the charitable contributions of the Church.

This latter duty deserves some comment, because this is the point where we may very well wish to think of new forms in which the concern might be expressed. Robert Browne, the sixteenth-century Separatist, called the deacons "Relievers," "a person having office of God to provide, gather and bestow the gifts and liberality of the Church, as there is need."[23] We might set a more modern passage beside this, as we see the United Presbyterian Church in the U.S.A. translating this concern into contemporary terms:

> The board of deacons shall minister to those in need, to the sick, to the friendless, and to any who may be in distress, in accordance with the Scriptural duties of the office. There may be delegated to the board of deacons, under the direction of the session, certain specifically designated responsibilities relating to the development of the grace of liberality in the members of the church, to the devising of effective methods of collecting gifts of the people, to the finances and properties of the church, and to its evangelistic, missionary, and educational program.[24]

This is a good statement, for it reflects the New Testament's concern that the Church should share its material benefits and provide modern forms in which it can be expressed. Indeed, it illustrates the fact that, in our modern understanding of the deacon's task, we must think of the Church's compassion reaching out to the whole world. If we are to think in terms of a modern diaconate, we shall have to take into account the work of the deacons and deaconesses of European Protestantism, the Fraternal Workers, and those in Christian relief organizations, the members of the new Protestant religious orders that are springing up, and the medical, educational, and agricultural missionaries. The whole social and compassionate outreach of the Church is the expression of the Church's *diakonia*. This is certainly not to rule out the work of local diaconates or to regard them as unnecessary, but simply to suggest that we need to supplement their work and witness at a time when we are increasingly forced to recognize that the work of the Church is one throughout the world.

The local diaconate emphasizes one thing which more scattered forms might find more difficult to express. This is the unity between service and sacrament. There is certainly some significance in the fact that, in the person of its deacons, a Protestant church recognizes the ministry of its laity by giving them special duties at its central sacrament. But far beyond this, in taking the Bread and Wine and distributing them to the people, the deacon gives visible testimony to the fact that the *diakonia* of the *whole* Church draws its strength and takes its character from the sacrament of Broken Bread and Poured-out Wine. The ministry of service is our calling. This is the place where the Church corporately prepares itself for its ministry to the world, and this is the place where leadership can be shown only in service.

4. There is one insight from the figure of the deacon in the New Testament which has not been emphasized by the Church, Protestant or Catholic, except by a few evangelicals. If the deacons of the New Testament trace their origin to the appointment of the Seven in Acts 6,[25] it is clear that beyond the formal duties connected with their appointment, they gave leadership to the Church in witness and evangelism. Stephen and Philip in some ways deserve to be regarded as the men who initiated the Church's missionary expansion.

It is sometimes forgotten, however, that until Protestantism came under the influence of the great evangelical revivals, it was not seriously interested in evangelizing outside its own borders,[26] and by that time the arguments about scriptural polities had become fixed into a very definite mold. It is surprising, nonetheless, that when the Disciples revived concern about church polity as an *expression* of evangelism in the nineteenth century, the connection between the New Testament deacons and the Church's missionary outreach was missed. Perhaps it was because the deacon was, to them, so obviously an officer of the local church, or because they had already drawn such clear lines between their own preachers (pastors) and the evangelical mission of the apostles.

In the modern period of church history, possibly the best example of the primitive diaconate at work in evangelism is the work of the Baptist lay preachers and churches as they traveled westward to the American frontier. Historian William Warren Sweet wrote:

> The typical Baptist preacher on the frontier was a settler who worked on his land five or six days each week, except when called upon to hold week-day meetings or funerals. . . . There were two types of frontier Baptist preachers, *licensed* and *ordained*, and sometimes there were several ministers in a congregation, though generally one was designated as pastor of the flock. Licensing a preacher was the first step in the making of a minister after he had been permitted to "exercise his gifts" by vote of the church. When chosen to take charge of a regular congregation he was then ordained.[27]

What we call the office of such lay preachers is immaterial. In their evangelical zeal, in their practical concern to keep work on the farm and work in the Church together, they were truly representative of the Church's *diakonia*. They remind us that one of the most certain duties of the deacon in the New Testament was his call to witness to the faith. This should remain in the forefront of any deacon's call to serve, whether he exercises his ministry in the comparatively restricted society of his own home town, or in some wider sphere of action, for he is representative of the Church's ministry *in* the world, a representative of the mission of the whole people of God in the society within which God has placed him.

Implicitly, we have already raised the question whether the traditional forms in which the order of deacons appears in our churches are adequate to meet the needs of our contemporary world. Boards of deacons connected with local congregations can fulfill a vital role in the life and witness of that local church, but if we are concerned with Christian service in its widest application, is not the way open to develop many forms, and is not there scope for the exercise of many differing gifts? The United Presbyterian Church in the U.S.A. seems to be breaking from the traditional Protestant idea of a deacon when it suggests that "a deacon is a minister who serves the Church with the permission of the presbytery beyond the bounds of a local congregation. He is assigned to duties that are primarily evangelistic or administrative. The presbytery may authorize him to bear rule in the presbytery."[28] This, and another lengthy passage in *The Nature of the Ministry*, is an indication of the way in which one Protestant denomination is prepared to think about an old question—the diaconate—in a new way.[29] But the accent is upon a form of the diaconate in which it will be an order of *ordained* ministry.

I would have to place a question mark at this point, not because the issue has been decided otherwise—indeed, we have to recognize that, in all the Catholic branches of the Church, the office is always an order of the ordained clergy—but because I question whether the *ordination* of deacons best expresses the ecumenical doctrine of the Church that seems to be emerging from our understanding of biblical theology. I suggest it was insight and not stupidity that caused the Puritans to make the deacon's office an essentially *lay* office in the Church, because in that office they were emphasizing at one and the same time the call of the layman to exercise a true churchly *ministry*, and also his responsibility to exercise that call specifically in the ministry of compassion and service.

Today we are searching for new ways in which the corporate mission of the People of God can be made real to the Church's membership; we want to discover new forms by which the leadership, which exists among us in many forms of endeavor, could be recognized by the Church and dedicated to its service; we wish to recognize the true vocation of those men and women who know themselves called to be *lay*, and who at the same time know themselves called also by God to carry out a very real ministry of compassion in the name of Christ, in the Church and in the world.

Perhaps a new order of deacons could be such a vehicle. If we could strip from our traditional ideas the prejudices born of literalism or convention, and concentrate upon that essential ministry of the living Christ which the New Testament deacon expressed to the Church in his own generation, then we might recapture an idea of the diaconate that would be relevant to our world. Such deacons might be able to speak that contemporary word which the Church needs to speak, for their ministry would be cast in the mold of the one and only essential ministry, the ministry of the Incarnate Servant who went regularly to the synagogue to worship, and in the strength of that faith gave himself to the service of man in the highways and byways of the secular world.

NOTE

Since this chapter was written in the Spring of 1965 a good deal has happened to reinforce some of the views which I then put forward. In particular, I have been intrigued to see how far those views coincided with the suggestions made in the Consultation on Church Union's *Principles of Church Union* [Forward Movement Publications (Cincinnati, Ohio, 1966)]. Having admitted that "much further study is required for a clear delineation of this office," the compilers go on to say: "Deacons should be given a share in the conduct of public worship and thus be enabled to exemplify, by their activity within the congregation as in the world, the interdependence of worship and service, and the encounter between the word of the Gospel and the needs of the world" (p 53). I believe it is this relationship that the Protestant Churches have tried historically to maintain within this office.

JOSEF HORNEF

THE ORDER OF DIACONATE IN THE ROMAN CATHOLIC CHURCH

Christ, our High priest, conferred on the apostles the fullness of the priestly office and, at the same time, entrusted its administration to the Church. This meant that the apostles, and the bishops as their successors, could, using this supreme power of administration, confer their office on others, either in full or in part. Thus, they ordained priests with specifically sacerdotal functions, and they ordained deacons with specifically diaconal, or ministering, functions. Leaving aside the moot point as to whether the seven men mentioned in the Acts of the Apostles were really deacons in the fullest sense, we can state definitely that the pastoral epistles of St. Paul speak of the office of *episcopos*, and the office of deacon distinct from it. The diaconate is therefore a biblically attested office.

The Roman Catholic Church's Code of Canon Law says in canon 108 that, *by virtue of divine institution*, the sacred hierarchy consists, on the basis of orders (*ratione ordinis*), of bishops, priests, and *ministri*; under this latter term we are to understand deacons; it asserts accordingly that the diaconate is also an office of divine right, but this by no means contradicts what we have said above. Karl Rahner explains the point in the following way:

There is no reason to hold that the threefold division of office in the Church (the episcopal, sacerdotal, and diaconal offices) goes back directly to the express will of the historical Jesus, expressly stated either before or after the Resurrection. But this is not to deny the *jus divinum* of these three grades of office. We can state quite definitely without fear of error that Jesus gave the priestly office to the Church with a provision for these three offices, in other words, he gave to the College of Apostles, with Peter at its head, all the power, authority, commissions, and rights which followed necessarily from the nature of the newly founded Church or such as he had himself expressly declared to be necessary for the Church. And with the foundation of the Church as a perfect society, the priestly office in the Church was given also the right to confer the power of this office on others, either in full or to a limited extent, according to the practical necessities of time and place.[1]

THE PLACE OF THE DEACON IN THE CHURCH

The diaconate is the lowest stage of the sacrament of Orders. By ordination the deacon is given a special mission in the Church; he is endowed with a specific grace belonging to his office and an indelible character is imprinted on his soul, which we may describe as a charismatic likeness to Christ, the first Deacon, who came not to be ministered unto, but to minister. At his ordination he ceases to be a layman and belongs to the hierarchy, to the *ordo sacer*. The three degrees of office in the early Church—bishop, priest, and deacon—are described by Leo the Great and by St. Benedict as the *ordo sacerdotalis*, and the very prayers of the rite of ordination to the diaconate show how near the office of the deacon is to that of the priest. We are guilty, therefore, of no heresy in describing the office of the deacon as a priestly office in the broader sense.

The Apostolic Constitution of Nov. 30, 1947 declares the essential part of the rite of ordination (the "form" of the ordination) to be the imposition of hands and the Preface, or more exactly, the invocation of the Holy Spirit which is contained in this prayer. Ordination to the diaconate is preceded by the minor orders and the subdiaconate. The obligation of celibacy is undertaken with the subdiaconate (canon 132). According to canon 973, the order of deacon can be conferred only on those who intend to become priests. Thus the Catholic Church's law states that the diaconate is *only a preparatory stage*, or a transition stage, *on the way to the priesthood*. [For the change in this law, effected by the *motu proprio* of Paul VI (June 27, 1967), see below.]

Ordination to the diaconate can be conferred only on one who has completed his 22nd year, ordination to the priesthood only on the completion of the 24th year. Between the two there is supposed to be an *interstitium* or interval of three months, but often this interval is of six months or more.[13]

THE FUNCTIONS OF THE DEACON

According to the prayers of the rite of ordination, the deacon must serve the altar, baptize, and preach. It is his function, therefore, to assist the priest at the Holy Sacrifice in the manner laid down in the liturgical books. The words *comminister et cooperator corporis et sanguinis Domini*, used in the rite of ordination, express his diaconal service of the Eucharist, and are a tribute to the lofty dignity of his ministering office, but they do not, of course, in any way imply that it is he who offers, or in theological past-tridentine terminology, "confects," the Holy Sacrifice. This offering is the function *of the priest alone*, who is the *minister ordinarius* of the sacraments, and in particular the sole minister of the sacrament of Penance. These, then, are the important differences between the priest and the deacon, differences which are clearly perceived and understood by the ordinary faithful.

To enumerate in detail the functions allotted to the deacon by the Church's code of laws, they are as follows: he is the *minister extraordinarius* of solemn Baptism and of Holy Communion, that is to say, he may in exceptional cases, with the permission of the bishop or the pastor (*licentia justa de causa concedenda*), administer solemn Baptism and likewise (*gravi de causa*) distribute Holy Communion (canons 741, 845). He may "expose" the Blessed Sacrament on the altar for the adoration of the faithful, but only the priest can give the benediction with the Blessed Sacrament (1274). He may preach (1342) and give certain blessings (1147), and above all, he may officiate at the burial ceremony.

When the bishop says, in the ceremony of ordination to the diaconate, "Receive this white stole from the hand of God. Fulfill thy ministry. . . ," the hearer finds himself involuntarily asking where this ministry is to be fulfilled, because, as a matter of fact, the diaconate in the Catholic Church had, for centuries, ceased to be a real office.[3] In exceptional cases the deacon might, in the short time that intervened between his ordination to the diaconate and his ordination to the priesthood, be given an opportunity to preach or baptize in his home town, or in the place where his seminary was situated. Generally, however, there is no longer any question of an office that was really exercised. Ordination to the diaconate and the brief time during which he enjoys the power of the office of deacon mark only a period of transition on the way to the final goal—priesthood.[4]

THE TRAINING OF THE DEACON

It might be fitting to comment at this point on the hitherto accepted practice in the Roman Catholic Church with regard to the training of the deacon. Since the diaconate has heretofore been merely a preparatory stage on the way to the priesthood, the training and formation of the deacon (insofar as one can speak of such a thing at all) has been merely a part of the training and formation of the future priest. The Church's Code of Canon Law lays down in canon 976 that ordination to the diaconate may take place only after the beginning of the fourth year of theological study.

According to canon 972, young people who wish to re-

ceive Holy Orders should have been received into a seminary
a teneris annis—from earliest youth. In fact, in many parts of
the world minor seminaries exist for boys of tender years, even
as young as ten, though they may enter at a later age. Such
minor seminaries impart a general training in the humanities,
after which the major seminaries offer training in philosophy
and theology. In this system, in force in many countries, a vast
majority of vocations to the priesthood, if not all of them, come
from the minor seminary. In other countries (Germany among
them) the minor seminary system is operated only by some
orders of the regular clergy. Vocations to the priesthood come
mainly from the high schools or colleges. After graduation from
such institutions, the young priest-to-be enters the ecclesiastical
seminary at the age of 19 or 20 and studies at the theological
faculty of the state university or, if there is no university with a
faculty of Catholic theology in the particular place, he may
study at the seminary's own school of theology and philosophy.
Up to ordination to the diaconate, the young candidate for
priesthood studies philosophy and theology, while after it he
continues the study of theology up to ordination to the priesthood and, in some places, even remains for some time in the
seminary after becoming a priest in order to complete his
training, particularly the practical aspects. The entire philosophi-
cal and theological training of our deacon, therefore, takes from
four to six years. (The program outlined here naturally admits
of regional variations.)

THE DIACONATE AND THE COUNCIL OF TRENT

Even as far back as the Council of Trent, an attempt was made
to give new life to the minor orders, the subdiaconate and the
diaconate.[5] In canon 17 of the Decree of June 15, 1563, it was
laid down that the functions corresponding to the various offices
from diaconate down to ostiariate should be exercised once
again. There was to be no longer any reason for people of
other faiths to look on the holders of these offices as idlers and

parasites (*tamquam otiosae*). The idea, then, was to revitalize the office. In this connection, the Council decreed that these functions should be carried out only by those who had received the corresponding orders. If there were not enough clerics available (i.e., candidates for the priesthood) to carry out the functions of those in minor orders, then the minor orders could be conferred on married people, who had proved themselves to be of blameless life; they would be suitably remunerated. Here, then, we have coming to the fore the idea of making the minor orders once again independent offices.

A draft decree, proposed to the Council on July 6, 1563, *Canones reformati abusum de sacramento ordinis*, went into this point in some detail. The authors of this draft had added new functions to the traditional functions of these various orders, with a view to making them more viable. It was declared that the diaconate was clearly distinct from all other offices in the Church, and that, of all offices, it stood nearest to the priesthood (*sacerdotio proximus*). It was stated that the service of the deacon was so important that the Church should never be without it. The draft decree stressed, along with the various liturgical functions of the deacon, his ministry to the widows, children, and orphans, the sick, the imprisoned, and all in distress, and emphasized that his care was to be not only for their bodily welfare, but also for their spiritual progress. "For all these they must have an open mind and an indefatigable zeal. For their ardent love must encompass all the faithful, especially those who are most sorely in need of the helping hand of love."[6] The draft decree, in this detailed form, did not become law, but its terms show quite clearly that its authors were only too well aware of the needs of the times. The decree, as finally issued on July 15, 1563, is more or less along the same lines, but this same Council also obliged bishops to have their priests trained in seminaries, and this gives us a clue as to why the proposed reform of the minor orders never got beyond the blueprint stage.

The demands of seminary life came to mean, in practice,

that the candidate for the priesthood could exercise the powers of the various orders as they were conferred on him only in the immediate vicinity of his place of study, or perhaps while at home on vacation, but never for a very long time. And this was just not enough for the reintroduction of the various offices, particularly that of the deacon, into the Church.

After the Council, it was decided, on second thought, that it might be better, after all, not to confer minor orders on married laymen, as it might seem to those of the Reformed faith that the Roman Catholic Church was beginning to yield ground on the question of clerical celibacy; thus, everything remained as it was before. In view of this, it is interesting to note that, in the period of crisis which the post-Reformation years brought to the Catholic Church in Germany, the official visitor of the Society of Jesus in Germany, Fr. Jerome Nadal, acting with the consent of the Provincial, Fr. Peter Canisius, wrote to the Father General of the order, Fr. Francis Borgia, in 1566, asking him to petition the Holy Father to introduce into Germany the system of uniting several parishes, entrusting them to one of the good priests who had remained loyal, and to compensate for the loss of manpower by assigning married clerics in minor orders to these priests as assistants. This, as we can see, is the same thought that had motivated the draft decree of Trent, mentioned above, but nothing was done about the suggestion.[7]

THE REVIVAL OF THE IDEA OF THE DIACONATE AFTER WORLD WAR II.

By the end of the nineteenth century and more and more so in the twentieth, a pastoral situation developed that created many great difficulties for the Church. One of the most tangible reasons for this state of emergency in the care of souls was a shortage of priests, particularly in Latin America, where dioceses and parishes are generally so vast. In mission territories, as well, the shortage was positively critical; in fact, missions ground to a stop for this very reason. The most obvious remedy was to replace missionaries by native clergy as soon as possible, but this was very often almost impossible. Furthermore, even in countries where Christianity was long-established, a shortage of priests made itself felt to a greater or lesser degree.

All this naturally led to the question as to some means of helping priests who are too few in number and therefore overburdened. This was chief among the several considerations that led to a demand for a revival of the diaconate. This demand came from various quarters independently, and became more urgent as time went on.[8] The Church was petitioned from many sides to restore the *diaconate as an independent office;* that is to say, in such a fashion that a man could become a deacon with the intention of remaining in that state all his life. I would like to mention only two of the many sources from which this call for the restored diaconate came. The first was the concentration camp of Dachau. The priests interned there were accustomed to discuss various questions relating to their calling, such as the training of priests, and so on, and one of the questions that arose was precisely this question of the revival of the diaconate. The two men who went into the question most deeply were the late Father Pies, S.J., and Father Schamoni, still happily alive in the ministry in Helmeringhausen in Sauerland. The fruit of these discussions was set down by Father Schamoni, which he managed to have smuggled out of Dachau. In an article in the magazine *Stimmen der Zeit* (October, 1947), "Block 26: Experiences in the Life of a Priest in Dachau," Father Pies mentioned these discussions in Dachau, and the brief reference to the revival of a diaconate made a deep impression on the present writer, who had lived in the* diaspora in Upper Hessen for 13 years, having been resettled there by the Nazis, and who therefore had firsthand experience of pas-

---

* *Translator's note*: The term "Diaspora," used several times throughout the article, is the German term for overwhelmingly non-Catholic areas of Germany with small Catholic communities. The term is used rather loosely—my experience is that an area where roughly twenty per cent or less of the population is Catholic qualifies for the designation.

toral needs in this area. He begged Father Pies to publish something more on this question, but as the priest was unable to do so, the present author began to write about the matter himself. His early work on the subject was published at the end of 1949 in the magazine *Die Besinnung* of Nuremberg, and the whole question was opened up.

A second set of circumstances furthered discussion of the revival of the diaconate. After World War I, a group of young men in the training school for social workers, conducted by the German Catholic Social Services Conference at Freiburg in Breisgau, had decided that, for the furtherance of their social and charitable work, which was, after all, a diaconal function, the Church should confer on them ordination to the diaconate. This step would sanctify the work they were striving to carry out in the spirit of the Gospel, and bring a blessing on them and on the whole Church. The vision of the diaconate they at first glimpsed was mainly focused on the charitable work of the deacon, but in the course of time, and after earnest thought, they came to appreciate and to long for the diaconate in its very fullest meaning. From this beginning in Freiburg there arose other groups who made the diaconate their goal and who prepared themselves under the guidance of a priest spiritual director for the day when they might attain this goal; in fact, they even prepared their families for the necessary adjustment to this step. As of 1967, about 50 of these young men, from all walks of life, had thus placed themselves at the Church's disposal. In recent times, a similar group has been founded in France.

It is astonishing how soon the question of the diaconate began to be discussed in all its details and aspects in a comprehensive international literature, mainly magazine articles and monographs.[9] In 1962 Karl Rahner, in collaboration with Herbert Vorgrimler of Freiburg, edited *Diaconia in Christos A Revival of the Diaconate*. From the very beginning, Father Rahner had taken a positive stand in favor of the movement and had actively promoted it.

In this compendium, twenty-seven priests and a layman dealt with the problems created by a revival of the diaconate from the historical, theological, and practical aspects. In the same year, the diaconate groups, mentioned in the preceding paragraph, sent a petition to all the bishops of the world, and presented the results of their studies and reflections on the problem in a book, *And They Imposed Hands on Them with Prayer*.

WHAT DOES THIS REFORM WANT?

Did the advocates of a revival of the diaconate really think that such a revival was possible, and what did they hope from it?

A rebirth of the diaconate obviously would not institute something completely new; neither would it be a mere reconstruction of the system of the past, exactly as it was then, and simply because it did once exist. The Church is placed in the middle of history and must work out its mission of salvation as best it can at every moment of history—but history is in a constant state of flux and no one historical time is exactly the same as another. Nevertheless, certain parallels and points of comparison can be discerned between any two historical eras. If we assert that the Church, today, has much in common with the Church of early times, we are not to be thought desirous of slavishly imitating the practices of that early Church, or of luxuriating in a sort of "early Church Romanticism." When we point to the distressing condition of the pastoral ministry in many places today, to the shortage of priests, and to the excessive burdens on the few priests that there are, we are speaking quite soberly of practical matters. The Würzburg University expert on pastoral theology, H. Fleckenstein, in his article, "The Pastoral Possibilities of the Diaconate in German-Speaking Lands," offers a very revealing study of the difficulties currently besetting the pastoral ministry (and that, not in Latin America or in mission lands, but in Germany itself).[10]

What was at issue was the problem of providing the priest with a really valuable helper, who could be at his side in all areas, even in the sanctuary. This helper should not be just the pastor's errand boy nor the general *factotum* of the parish. He is the pastor's collaborator, his colleague in the ministry. In the early days of the Church, the deacon's function was seen as threefold: the service of the Eucharist, the service of the Word, and the service of his fellow-man; and the Church's law still recognizes this threefold service as the characteristic feature of the deacon's office, even if it often, in practice, restricts his opportunity to carry it out. This threefold service will remain the function of the deacon, but it will have to be re-phrased in a form suitable to the age—the deacon will serve through the liturgy, he will preach and catechize, he will help through social and charitable work for youth, he will counsel in family problems, he will assist the aged and the sick.

It would not be possible, here, to map out a detailed program for the modern deacon; a few thoughts must suffice. It belongs to the deacon's office to serve in charity all who need his help, and to give that service in the form of modern pastoral care, but this care and love and service must have its source at the altar. In the person of the deacon, all this is made possible—he comes from the altar to the people with his service of charity in the same way that he brings the message of the Word to the people from the altar. He can help with house-to-house visitation, with family counseling, with the guidance of the newly-wed, and with premarriage counseling for engaged couples—in fact, if he is a married man, he will be particularly qualified for this work. He can bring Communion more frequently to the sick, at home or in hospitals. He can take over many religious instruction classes from the pastor, and so on. In this way the overburdened pastor can be relieved of some of his load, and the work of the ministry can be extended and deepened. There would be also special assignments with which the deacon could be entrusted—why, for instance, should we not have the worker-deacon, that is to say, the manual worker ordained to the diaconate. Just like the priest, the deacon must derive his strength from the liturgy; he should approach the altar with the priest every day, so far as this is possible, in the *Missa cum diacono*.

THE DIACONATE AT THE SECOND VATICAN COUNCIL

The whole question of the diaconate certainly would not have come to the forefront so quickly, had Vatican Council II not provided it with a golden opportunity.[11]

The Council may be said broadly to have set itself two purposes: the one, pastoral, the other, ecumenical. In its search for practical means of combating the state of distress in pastoral affairs, in its efforts to come to grips with the fundamental nature and mission of the Church, the Council was bound to run into the question of the diaconate and, to its credit, it did not shirk that responsibility. The basic proposition that emerged was that every office in the Church entails service. The Church was sent to serve. This is true even of the office of the pope, who is called the *servus servorum Dei*. What of the deacon? Should not the idea of service be represented at its very finest in him, if he is to be true to his name, which means literally "servant," or "minister"?

In the draft decree *De Ecclesia*, the Theological Commission had devoted a few lines only to the office of deacon, but these few lines were sufficient to make it, we may say without fear of exaggeration, an issue of the foremost importance at the second session. No less than 36 cardinals and bishops spoke on the question, for and against. A number of Fathers were completely opposed to the diaconate, while some rejected only the married diaconate. The Italian cardinals and bishops, in particular, could not reconcile themselves to the prospect of a revival of the diaconate. Other Fathers made an urgent appeal for a chance to revive the diaconate, because they needed it so urgently. They begged the Fathers to keep their desperate position in mind, even if they, themselves, did not need the diaconate in their own dioceses or have the intention of permitting it. The European Cardinals, Julius Döpfner of Munich; Leo Suenens of Malines-Brussels; and Paul Richaud of Bordeaux, and also Cardinal Juan Ricketts of Lima, Peru, expressed themselves wholeheartedly in favor of the diaconate, as did the Ukrainian Metropolitan Josyf Slipyj. Cardinal Ricketts and three other Fathers, speaking for 164 Latin American bishops, were in favor, as were two Fathers from Asia, and one from West Africa, each one speaking for a large number of fellow prelates. A Portuguese bishop, representing 30 bishops, spoke against the married deacon. However, when the discussion was over, it was impossible to estimate whether a two-thirds majority in favor of the diaconate could be attained. (It is of interest to note that the vote on the collegiality of the bishops also defied the wisdom of the forecasters in the same way.) The preliminary voting on Oct. 30, 1963 was a great surprise. Although it was only after a long and thorny debate and only by a majority of one vote that the Presiding Committee decided to put the motion before the Council for a preliminary vote, the Council gave an overwhelming *approval in principle* to the restoration of the diaconate, with a majority that was only two votes short of a three-quarters majority. However, the question of whether the deacon should be married or celibate was left undecided, although the Theological Commission had not rejected the possibility of the married deacon, and had stated its view that the decision on this matter should be reserved to the Bishops, or to Episcopal Conferences, for the areas under their jurisdiction.

The diaconate was finally dealt with in the Third Session. The proclamation by Paul VI, on Nov. 21, 1964, of the Constitution *De Ecclesia* opened the door to the restoration of the diaconate as a permanent state. In view of the diversity of the situations prevailing in various places, this naturally did not mean a general restoration of the diaconate. It was quite clear all along that all the Council could do was to decide that the diaconate *could* be restored, wherever the conditions proved to be ripe for it. It should therefore be left to Episcopal Conferences to decide, with the approval of the Holy Father, whether the diaconate should be restored in their territories. The approval in principle of the restoration had won through, at any rate, with a majority of 1903 against 242.

It is of particular interest to examine the decision of the Council on the celibacy or otherwise of the deacon. The proposition put before the Council Fathers ran as follows: the decision shall rest with the supreme authority, i.e., the pope, as to whether: a) the diaconate may be conferred on *men of more mature years*, even though they be living in the married state; and b) whether it may also be conferred on suitable *younger men*, who will not be, thereby, bound to celibacy. Part a) was approved by 1,589 votes to 629, and was accordingly carried. Part b) was approved by 839 votes, but was turned down by 1,364, and was therefore lost. In the final vote on the diaconate on September 30, there were 1,704 votes for restoration, 53 against, and 481 who voted "in favor, but with reservations." The proposal was accordingly carried, and the votes "with reservations" made no difference to the final result.

The fact that the votes in favor rose from 1,588 to 1903, and the votes against decreased from 525 to 242 shows how the climate of opinion with regard to the diaconate had improved between the second and third sessions of the Council. The final proposition on the place and the function of the deacon was carried with an overwhelming majority (2,055 for, 94 against).

This is what the Constitution says about the diaconate:

> At a lower level of the hierarchy are deacons, upon whom hands are imposed "not unto the priesthood, but unto a ministry of service." For strengthened by sacramental grace, in communion with the bishop and his group of priests, they serve the people of God in the ministry of the liturgy, of the word, and of charity. It is the duty of the deacon, to the extent that he has been authorized by competent authority,

to administer baptism solemnly, to be custodian and dispenser of the Eucharist, to assist at and bless marriages in the name of the Church, to bring Viaticum to the dying, to read the sacred Scripture to the faithful, to instruct and exhort the people, to preside at the worship and prayer of the faithful, to administer sacramentals, and to officiate at funeral and burial services. Dedicated to duties of charity and of administration, let deacons be mindful of the admonition of Blessed Polycarp: "Be merciful, diligent, walking according to the truth of the Lord, who became the servant of all."

These duties, so very necessary for the life of the Church, can in many areas be fulfilled only with difficulty according to the prevailing discipline of the Latin Church. For this reason, the diaconate can in the future be restored as a proper and permanent rank of the hierarchy. It pertains to the competent territorial bodies of bishops, of one kind or another, to decide, with the approval of the Supreme Pontiff, whether and where it is opportune for such deacons to be appointed for the care of souls. With the consent of the Roman Pontiff, this diaconate will be able to be conferred upon men of more mature age, even upon those living in the married state. It may also be conferred upon suitable young men. For them, however, the law of celibacy must remain intact.[12]

These words of the Constitution are self-explanatory; however, a word on the question of marriage or celibacy for the deacon might not be out of place at this stage.

The text quoted above fell considerably short of the expectations of many—that this is not a purely personal opinion is shown by, among other things, the 839 votes cast at the Council *for* the young married deacon. The author of these lines has repeatedly and energetically advocated this form of the diaconate, while many others, among them, Schamoni, in his *Married Men as Ordained Deacons* (London, 1955 and 1962), have put forward the case for men who have proved their probity in their professional and married lives as candidates for the diaconate. We mention these in passing because it seems that the restriction under discussion may eventually lead to serious difficulties in the recruitment and training of deacons, and may make it more difficult for them to maintain their position. This applies, especially, to the deacon employed full time in the service of the Church; a man who has entered a particular profession or trade and enjoys some competence and standing in it will scarcely be willing to forego all that to work for the Church in a full-time capacity; the most he can be expected to do is to serve as a part-time deacon. But these misgivings, which we have only briefly outlined here, should not keep us from giving thanks to God and to the Fathers of the Council for the fact that we have the diaconate once again. It was indeed a history-making decision. It may, I think, be safely assumed that the chief reason for the restriction of which we speak was the fear that many young theology students would withdraw from the quest for the priesthood, and would transfer to the diaconal seminary; this fear would be supported by economic considerations.

With regard to the "men of mature years" (for which the Theological Commission also uses the term "mature married men"), Bishop Frotz, Auxiliary Bishop of Cologne, writes:

> Many will be thinking of old men and wondering if they really will be of much help in the pastoral ministry. But what is really meant is "mature men," men who have proved their integrity and worth in their professional and personal lives. And for this, as experience teaches, many men do not need even three decades of life.[13]

It should be mentioned here that the young celibate deacon will be, as a rule, a member of a religious order, or of a community of religious Brothers, or of a secular institute, since their chosen way of life commits them, in any case, to celibacy. This could be of great value in mission countries in attracting young native Christians to the vocation of the religious Brother. Where, however, the young celibate deacon is a man living in the world, it goes without saying that he must be chosen with much greater care for a variety of reasons.

THE TRAINING OF THE NEW DIACONATE

In an earlier part of this paper, we outlined the hitherto accepted practice of the Catholic Church in regard to the training of her deacons. We must now devote some thought to the training and formation of this new independent diaconate, for which we have been waiting so long. There is not very much of a general nature that can be said about this training, since conditions vary so much from place to place. The deacon, particularly the full-time deacon, must have a very thorough formation, yet he will not need a very deep or intensive training in philosophy or theology. His calling has a more practical turn than that of the priest, and so the course of training in the ecclesiastical seminary is not for him. Sacred Scripture and liturgy should be the main sources of his theological training; however, the aim should be, not to impart to him a vast amount of knowlegde about them, but rather to base his spiritual formation and development on them. This is not the place, however, to go into detail about his theological training. It is also important that he should have a knowledge of, and some skill in, social work, and in the care and guidance of youth.

The provisions of the Constitution would seem to call for diaconal seminaries for *young* men (of twenty years and upwards). It is possible, also, that we could see a partial return to the pre-Trent system of training, whereby the training of an individual candidate for diaconate could be entrusted to a priest experienced in pastoral work, or small groups could be entrusted to groups of priests. For the part-time deacon, who spends his day in the practice of his secular calling, it would seem that we will have to depend on evening, weekend, and holiday courses for his training, but these could be extended over a correspondingly longer period of time.

In the training of the full-time deacon, it would seem wise to make use at first, as far as possible, of already existing institutions. In places, for instance, where there are training centers for catechists and social workers and other people whose work is Church-centered, so to speak, or such as to bring them into close contact with the Church, the years spent in training, and subsequently in the practice of the calling in question, will be sufficient to ensure the maturity and the personal uprightness to be expected of the deacon. A time will probably come, however, when a special institute will have to be set up for the training of the full-time deacon in view of the widely diverging backgrounds and qualifications of those who will come forward to offer themselves for the diaconate. There is no need here to specify the manner of the training in such an institute except to say that it must be sufficiently flexible and many-sided to serve all needs—in any case, experience will show what will be necessary.

This diaconal training will often be dependent on material help from outside, but this is not so much of a problem as in former times. We have only to think of the enormous amount of help given to Latin America by the annual "Adveniat" collection in Germany and other such efforts elsewhere. We know, also, of the system whereby priests and catechists in mission countries and other such areas are "adopted" by individuals, public bodies, parishes, and so on, in the more well-to-do Christian countries, who thereby undertake responsibility for their material support. Why should there not also be such adoption schemes for deacons?

THE NECESSITY OF BOTH FULL–TIME AND PART–TIME DIACONATE*

Continuity and undivided attention to the work of the ministry are essential features of all ecclesiastical office, and the higher

* *Translator's note*: The terms "hauptberuflicher Diakon" and "nebenberuflicher Diakon" are quite easy to understand, but difficult to translate. They mean, respectively, the man who practices no other calling except the diaconate and the man who has a secular profession or trade, and who acts as a deacon only in his spare time. I find the terms I have used, "part-time deacon" and "full-time deacon," not too easy on the ear, but I could not think of any better.

the office, the truer this is. Nevertheless, the Church just cannot do without the part-time deacon. Schamoni was the first to point out how valuable the work of the deacon can be in the mission station or in the chapel-of-ease in holding the congregation together, where there is no priest. Today we are coming more and more to recognize the value of the Sunday divine service without a priest. There can be no denying the difference between the service held by the ordained deacon and a service conducted by a layman, however zealous—the deacon can announce and explain the Word of God with greater authority and can distribute Holy Communion. It will be an economic impossibility to place a full-time deacon in each mission station or out-church which is without a priest, but in any case, a part-time deacon will generally be adequate. But even where the pastor has his center of operations, there, too, the part-time deacon will be able to render valuable services, even though he will have only his free time to put at the disposal of the Church. It would obviously be a very desirable thing if two or three part-time deacons could be found in the same place, who could take turns at the work of ministry, since their work for God must not be at the expense of their families.

Neither, however, can the Church do without the full-time deacon. He will be the sheet-anchor of this entire new institution which we have described; he will be the rock of strength, on which the part-time deacon will often depend for support and help. Even from the point of view of the amount of work he is able to accomplish, he will be worth much more, since he will be able to devote all his time and all his interest to the service of the Church, not to mention the fact that he will generally have had a much more thorough training. On the other hand, the Church will have to guarantee him a suitable family wage, and will have to look after his wants all his life. Anyone who is inclined to deplore the financial strain that this will impose upon the Church should reflect that, if priests were available in sufficient numbers to eliminate the need for the diaconate, they also would have to be supported. In short, the economic and social standing of the deacon must be in accordance with his station as a collaborator in the care of souls. We might mention here, too, that we will need the full-time deacon to act as director of all kinds of charitable institutions, a practice which has been common in the Protestant Churches for over a century. Further, the cooperation of his wife in this work could be of great value.

ARE DEACONS ALSO NEEDED IN COUNTRIES WHERE CHRISTIANITY HAS BEEN LONG ESTABLISHED?

Is it only in Latin America or in the mission countries that the diaconate is to be revived, or should it be revived, also, in the older Christian countries? Our thanks are due to Cardinals Richaud and Suenens for emphasizing that we need the deacon in these latter countries as well. We need him in the big cities, we need him in the Diaspora; we can make good use of him everywhere. It would be a mistake to see in the current worldwide shortage of priests the only reason for the restoration of the diaconate, though it is this factor that triggered the movement towards restoration of the diaconate. The ultimate reasons lie at a much deeper level. It was Cardinal Suenens who gave due prominence to the supernatural aspect of the question. The diaconate is an essential part of the Church's hierarchy, and to reject it would be to set aside an institution willed by God Himself. The Christian community has a right to the flow of grace, of which God has willed that the diaconate should be a channel; it has a right to receive the Eucharist and to hear the Word of God, and if this is not possible without the deacon, then the Christian community has a right to the restoration of the diaconate. And, indeed, it must be admitted that in those countries where Christianity has been long established, the pastoral ministry is sometimes, and in some places, rather behind the times, especially where the more modern forms of pastoral work are concerned, such as family guidance, pre-marriage counseling, and house-to-house visitation. These theological reasons for the revival of the diaconate are not bound by any considerations of time or place, but are of equal validity everywhere and always. To sum up, then, we need the deacon as a bridge and as a link between priest and people, between altar and congregation, between liturgy and life, between the Eucharist and the ministry of charity.

THE MOTU PROPRIO OF POPE PAUL VI

If the deliberations of Vatican II opened the door to the full restoration of the diaconate, as mentioned above, Pope Paul VI took the definitive step in his *motu proprio* of Jan. 27, 1967. This document provides for the creation of two new kinds of permanent deacons: young men, at least twenty-five years of age, who have completed the special three-year training course and who will be bound by the traditional celibacy requirements; men, at least thirty-five years of age, who have received an abbreviated training program, and who may be married before, but not after their ordination as deacons.

When and where this program gets under actual way, the new permanent deacons are to be ordained in the same manner as seminarians who become deacons while preparing for the priesthood. It is envisioned that the ceremony will be modified later by the Holy See. The document states that the younger deacons will attend a special institute where they will be tested, taught to live a truly evangelical life, and prepared to develop a specific function. Their course of study will last at least three years, and will include, not only doctrine, but practical instruction in such subjects as teaching, public speaking, and pastoral visitation. The older deacons will be "admitted for certain time in a special institute" or, if this is not possible, placed under the care of some "priest of eminent virtue"; if they are married, they can become deacons only with the consent of the wife. After ordination, all deacons will be "unable to marry." The document further suggests that older deacons would or could continue to practice their previous professions, but it stipulates that these must not "conflict with or impede fruitful practice of holy ministry."

This restoration of the diaconate as a permanent state, whether for the unmarried younger deacons or the married older deacons, is not completely automatic. The episcopal conference or body of bishops in each country must seek the approval of the Holy See, and indicate "the reasons that lead it to put the new discipline into effect." It is to be anticipated that countries where there is no serious shortage of priests, such as the United States, will not move as quickly to the full implementation of this *motu proprio* as will other countries in Latin America and Asia, for example, where deacons are greatly needed to relieve the shortage of priests, and the burdens on the priests who are now functioning. After 1,000 years of comparative neglect, however, Paul VI has taken the definitive step toward restoring the diaconate to its original dignity and glory, and thus given concrete proof to the world that the order is by no means outmoded, as indeed it could never have been, because it is a sacred order.

THE ECUMENICAL ASPECTS OF THE DIACONATE

The lively interest that has been awakened everywhere in this question of the restoration or the reform of the diaconate is most remarkable. In the Evangelical (Protestant) Church in Germany, efforts are under way to make the deacon like the pastor, the holder of an ecclesiastical office, and to devise an appropriate ordination rite for him as against the present system whereby he merely receives a blessing from his brotherhood of deacons and is thus sent to the congregation among whom he will be working. Many want also to see him take a greater part in the celebration of the liturgy, instead of being exclusively concerned with social and charitable work for the congregation, as is today mainly the case. (It seems certain that the deacon at the altar would have a much greater appeal than the "woman pastor.") The German Protestant Brotherhood of St. Michael made the diaconate the theme of their 1964 conference, and the World Council of Churches had a symposium, *Nine Points on the Office of the Diaconate in the Church*, published in 1964 by its Commission on Faith and Order working in collaboration with its Laymen's Union. This symposium, which shows the great interest being taken in the progress of thought on this question, follows on reports from the Episcopal Church in the United States that several bishops have made practical, and highly successful, experiments towards a revitalization of the diaconate. All these developments point to a new common interest between the Catholic and Protestant Churches. Before we come together at the Table of the Lord, is there any reason why the deacons of both confessions should not come together and work side by side on practical projects of Christian charity, and, thus, working in harmony, fulfill the word of the Lord: "Whatsoever you have done to the least of my brethren, you have done it to Me"!

GEORGES FLOROVSKY

THE PROBLEM OF DIACONATE IN THE ORTHODOX CHURCH

The scope of this chapter is limited. It is not our task here to discuss in detail the history of the diaconate in the Eastern Orthodox Church. We shall address ourselves to the contemporary situation, and the problems implied in it. On the other hand, this situation can be properly understood and appraised only in historic perspective. The diaconate has obviously changed its shape and function more than once in the course of history; hence, the Orthodox theologian is guided in his inquiry by tradition, especially in controversial matters. From early times the diaconate was acknowledged as an integral part of the threefold structure of apostolic ministry, if only in the third place. Strangely enough, the actual origin of the diaconate as an institution is still an open, and rather obscure, issue. It is generally assumed that the diaconate can be traced back to the appointment of the Seven by the apostles, described in the sixth chapter of the Book of Acts, although the name "deacons" does not appear in the text. This was the usual interpretation in the West, as early as the time of St. Irenaeus.

In modern times, however, this interpretation has been challenged. The Orthodox theologian is bound at this point to take into account that venerable exegetical tradition of which St. John Chrysostom was an authoritative exponent and witness. Speaking of the election of the Seven, in his homilies on the Book of Acts, Chrysostom emphatically and formally denies that Seven were "ordained" as deacons, for the simple reason that at that time no distinct ecclesiastical orders existed: no bishops, no presbyters, and no deacons. According to Chrysostom, the Seven were appointed for an occasional and specific task, that is, for the "service of tables" (*Acta Apostolorum*, hom. XIV, MG LX, c. 116). It may be argued that this interpretation simply reflected the situation in Chrysostom's own time, when the diaconate had become, especially in the East, a liturgical institution. Yet, Chrysostom in no way was inclined to minimize the importance of charitable *diakonia* in the Church; indeed, the social responsibility of the Church was one of his crucial concerns. He simply insisted that the diaconate was instituted in the Church for a different task and purpose.

Whatever may be said of Chrysostom's exegesis, it was authoritatively endorsed by the Council of Trullo (692), with direct reference to Chrysostom's witness. The question was raised whether it was permissible to have more than seven deacons in a given local Church. The local Council of Neocaesarea (*c.* 315) ruled that the pattern of the Seven had to be adhered to, with the reference to Acts (canon 15). The Council of Trullo, after having pondered the whole matter and, with direct reference to Chrysostom's witness, reversed the ruling, since there was no valid reason for limitation in number. Indeed, there was no identity or connection between the "liturgical diaconate," *ton tois mysteriois diakonoumenon andron*, and the *diaconia* of the Seven, which was restricted solely to the "service of tables." This "service," special and occasional, must remain, however, a "pattern of philanthrophy and charitable care," *typos philanthropias kai spoudes* (canon 16). This sharp distinction between the *hierourgias diakonia* and the *oikonomia ton trofon* became a commonplace of Byzantine canonical thinking.[1] It has been maintained by many competent scholars in the Russian Church in modern times, both by exegetes and by canonists.[2]

The order of deacons has always been regarded in Catholic tradition as a subordinate and subsidiary office in the total structure of ecclesiastical ministry: In the documents of the early Church deacons are usually described as "servants" or "attendants" of the bishop: *ton men episkopou hyperetai eisin,* in the phrase of the first Ecumenical Council (Nicaea I, A.D. 325, canon 18). They constituted at that time the working retinue, as it were, of the bishop, and in this capacity were assigned various tasks, primarily in the field of pastoral administration and service to the needy. The very term *diakonia* seems to have denoted at that time precisely this special kind of service. Deacons had a wide area of duties in the early Church, but a limited and subordinate competence. They acted by the bishop's authority and under his orders, and had to report all matters to him for decision. They were not supposed to do anything without his knowledge and approval, "in a clandestine way." As the bishop's agents and representatives, acting on his behalf and in his stead, they held an influential and distinguished position in the life of Christian communities. Accordingly, they were described sometimes not only as the bishop's "servants," but also as his "apostles and prophets," as his "ear and eye, mouth, heart, and soul" (*Apostolic Constitutions,* bk. II, ch. 30, 31, 32, 43).

In conjunction with that *hyperesia,* deacons had from early times their own distinctive role in the liturgical worship of the Church and were described also as "servants of Christ's mysteries" (St. Ignatius, Trallians 2). According to the *Apostolic Tradition* of Hippolytus, deacons were ordained by the imposition of hands by the bishop, not *in sacerdotio, sed in ministerio episcopi,* and for that reason presbyters, or priests, were not supposed to participate in the rite of ordination, since deacons were not their *symbouloi* and had no share of that spirit of counsel which was the common possession of "the clergy": *non est enim* [*diaconus*] *particeps consilii in clero* (*id.* 9). This sharp distinction between *sacerdotium* (common to bishops and priests) and *ministerium,* or *hyperesia,* is highly significant. Strictly speaking, according to the *Apostolic Tradition,* deacons did not belong to "clergy," *kleros,* at all.[3] On the other hand, their actual prominence in the practical field could but breed and encourage ambition and pride. As early as the Council of Nicaea, they had to be recalled to "their proper limits," *tois idiois metrois,* and to be reminded that their order was lower than that of the presbyters, *ton presbyteron elattous,* since they were no more than "bishop's servants" (canon 18, quoted above). The tension continued, however, and the Council of Trullo was compelled to wrestle with the same problem once more. Deacons were still, even at that time, appointed occasionally to certain administrative positions (*offikia ekklesiastika exontes*), and granted thereby "dignity" or "honor" (*axioma*). They tended therefore to assume precedence over presbyters. The Council dismissed all such claims as license and presumption (canon 7).

What is crucial and essential in this ruling is obviously the strict distinction between "order" and "office." The ruling implies that administrative appointments or commissions do not change the hierarchical status of the appointees, in spite of the *axioma* which such appointments may confer. Now, the question immediately arises: was the "service to the bishop," the *hyperesia,* just an "office"; that is, a "commission," and assigned task? And what exactly was the relation of such "commission" or task to the "order"? The early rites of ordination are rather vague at this point. They do not specify the *charisma* conferred by ordination to the diaconate, nor do they define those functions to which deacons are ordained. Yet, the subordinate and auxiliary character of the diaconate is clearly stated. The only clue here is, perhaps, the reference to St. Stephen, which occurs in the rite described in the eighth book of the *Apostolic Constitutions* "And replenish him with thy Holy Spirit, and with power, as thou didst replenish Stephen, thy martyr and the follower of the sufferings of thy Christ" (ch.

18). This clause is retained in the later Byzantine rite that is still in use. It is significant, however, that St. Stephen alone is mentioned here, and is mentioned as martyr and sufferer and not as "deacon." It is rather an analogy, with an emphasis on the charismatic character of service. In the course of time most of the tasks that originally constituted the *hyperesia* of deacons were transferred or reassigned to other agents. Indeed, the pastoral care, in general, and especially the care of the poor and needy, could be exercised by bishops in manifold ways and through diverse channels. Moreover, charity and mutual service was the obvious duty of all believers and of the whole community.

Of the various duties which characterized the service of deacons in the early Church, only their liturgical function, with special reference to the celebration of the holy Eucharist, has been retained as their distinctive and proper task. In a sense, it was a conspicuous change, but it would be inaccurate to describe it as an atrophy or decline of the diaconate. Indeed, it meant a reorganization of the Church's *diakonia* at large. It implied also a new interpretation of the nature of the diaconate, still in line with the old tradition, but with sharper distinction be tween "order" and various "offices" or commissioned tasks. In fact, the liturgical role of deacons was becoming increasingly conspicuous precisely in the fourth century, in the period of stabilization and unification of rites. It was for the role and function of "liturgical assistants" (of bishops *and* priests) that deacons were ordained. This was their basic and primary function, and it constituted their ecclesiastical and ministerial status.

In the contemporary rite of ordination to the diaconate its auxiliary character is clearly indicated. The ordination takes place at the liturgy after the *anaphora*, that is, after the consecration of the elements; and this is meant to signify that deacons do not take any *acting* part in the consecration, except insofar as the whole worshipping congregation also is supposed and invited to join in prayer and to share in this way in the celebration. On the contrary, ordination to priesthood takes place before the consecration, at the very beginning of the sacramental service, so that a newly ordained priest is able immediately to join the bishop and his fellow-presbyters in the priestly action of consecration. This twofold ordination is a new way to express the traditional distinction: deacons are ordained *in ministerio*, whereas priests are ordained *in sacerdotio*. After the rite of ordination has been completed, the new deacon receives from the bishop a *ripidion*, or *flabellum*, a kind of fan, with which he is supposed "to guard" the Sacrament (originally from flies and insects). Now it is no more than a symbolic gesture, but it expresses clearly the serving role of deacons in the liturgy of the Church. In modern times the *ripidia* are made in the shape of cherubs (and are accordingly called *hexapteryga*), in order to suggest an analogy between angels and deacons, since angels also are but "serving spirits." According to the contemporary rule, ordination to the diaconate may also be performed at the Liturgy of the Presanctified Gifts, which is not a sacramental service in the strict sense, but simply a special variant of Vespers with the additional rite of administering holy Communion from the presanctified, or reserved, Sacrament. In brief, deacons are not supposed or permitted to function as such, except as assistants of the officiating priest or bishop. They are no more than assistants.

The liturgical function of the deacon is conspicuous and impressive in the Eastern rite. Western liturgiologists usually regard it as a distinctive and most characteristic feature of this rite.[4] On the whole, this observation is correct; however, if the assistance or participation of deacons in the divine service is normal, regular, and desirable, it is not indispensable or obligatory, since it is an auxiliary and subsidiary function. This assistance belongs, as it were, to the *plene esse* of the liturgical rite, to its ceremonial completeness and perfection, rather than to its very *esse*. As a matter of fact, there are no deacons at all in the majority of Orthodox communities today. This may be a sign of crisis or decline, but it must be considered seriously and understood properly. It is significant that as early as the fourteenth century, the great Byzantine interpreter of the liturgical rites, Nicholas Cabasilas, was rather reticent about the function of deacons.

Let us turn now to the analysis of the rite itself. First of all, the deacon is a *keryx*, a kind of liturgical herald or crier. The term itself has been used by St. John Chrysostom and by Theodore of Mopsuestia.[5] The deacon announces the beginning of the service and invites the officiating priest to give the initial blessing or invocation (*kairos tou poiesai to kyrio*), while he himself receives the permission to start. The deacon exhorts the congregation to join in prayer, and at certain particular points he stirs its attention: *orfoi-proschomen*—"stand aright," "let us attend." It is his duty and privilege to call the congregation, before the *anaphora*, to recognize each other, "to love one another," and to introduce the recitation of the Creed. It is his privilege also to invite the celebrant to proceed to the consecration of gifts. It is his task to invite communicants to approach and to receive holy Communion from the hands of the officiating priest or bishop. It seems that in the ancient church deacons were permitted, or even commissioned, to administer communion themselves, if only to the lay people, and this is still occasionally done, mainly in the Greek Church, although it is now commonly regarded rather as an abuse. In all these instances the deacon appears to be the keeper of the liturgical order. The role of a herald is, by its very nature and purpose, conspicuous, but obviously it is auxiliary and subordinate. Lessons at the liturgy are normally read by deacons, although the epistle is usually read by an *anagnostes*, or even by a layman, and probably, in older times, it was the privilege of the *anagnostes* to read all lessons. Before the reading of the Gospel, the deacon asks for the blessing of the officiating priest in a rather solemn form.

The most significant function of the deacon in the divine rite is, no doubt, the recitation of the litanies, of which, in a sense, he is the regular minister. The litanies, however, may be said only in the context of the regular public service presided over by a priest (or bishop); outside of this context they cannot be said at all. The ministry of the deacon is in this case a subordinate ministry. It is hardly accurate to describe the litany as a dialogue for there are no replies, or answers. Nor is it accurate to describe the deacon as a leader of the congregation, or as a mediator between the priest and the congregation, as it is often done, especially by Western scholars.[6] As a matter of fact, the deacon does not recite prayers—that is, the litanies—on the behalf of the congregation; he only invites it to pray. "Let us pray" is simply an invitation, not yet the prayer itself. In the phrase of such a competent student of the Eastern rite as Jean Michel Hanssens, "both the celebrant and the people pray together in litanies, though in many different forms," and the clauses of the litany pronounced by the deacon "are exhortations directed to the people rather than prayers addressed to God."[7] Indeed, "to invite" is not the same as "to lead."

Each litany must be concluded with a doxology by the priest, who is actually the true and only leader of the congregation. It is proper at this point to quote the comments of Cabasilas: "*At the beginning the priest exhorts the people to prayer, for he is appointed to this office* and is for that reason placed in front of the people. *He is also their ambassador and mediator* (*os presbeutes auton kai mesites*). . . . After he has prayed for all his intentions, *the priest calls upon the faithful* to commend themselves to God."[8] Now, the litanies are recited by the deacon, and the priest has his own prayers to be said at the same time, *submissa voce*, within the sanctuary. There is an apparent duplication, or parallelism, of prayers; yet, the litany is incomplete without the doxology which can be given only by the priest. It is much more than just an audible exclamation (*ekfonesis*). In the phrase of Cabasilas, it is an explanatory verse (*akroteleutios*), which gives the reason for which prayers may be offered at all (*prostithesi ten aitian*). The reason is the glory of God. "*The priest wants to bring all the faithful to share in his hymn of praise . . . and the congregation do in-*

deed unite themselves to his prayer, for when he has recited the doxology, all the faithful say 'Amen,' and by this acclamation *they take to themselves as their own the prayers of the priest.*"[9]

It is hardly correct, therefore, to describe the deacon as an intermediary between the congregation and the officiating priest. Indeed, the priest, who has direct contact with the congregation, is himself their mediator. The prayers of the priest and of the congregation are not only coordinated, they are truly integrated into one action of praise and intercession. The role of the deacon is conspicuous, especially in the first part of the divine liturgy, the *enarxis*, but it would be a gross exaggeration to consider him as a minister in his own right. There is no reason to assume, as it has been sometimes suggested, that the duplication of prayers in the *enarxis* was motivated by the Semitic conception of the Holy as totally inaccessible to ordinary people.[10] Nor is it probable that this duplication had been introduced deliberately to secure the closer participation of the people in the worship, when language difficulties arose.[11] In any case, this does not apply to the Byzantine liturgy, in which the language of the people has been always used. It is important to underline that this duplication of prayers in the *enarxis* has nothing to do with the habit of reciting the *anaphora* in secret (*mystikos*). In this case, there is actually no duplication at all: the part of the prayer which is recited now by the priest "insecret," the parts of it audibly intoned by the priest, and the responses of the people, constitute in fact one single and continuous prayer, which is offered by the celebrating priest in the name and on behalf of the whole Church as gathered at that time for celebration, and in which both the celebrant and the congregation participate jointly, if *diversis modis*. The *anaphora* is indeed the *common prayer* of the Church, *publica et communis oratio*.[12] Characteristically, at this point the deacon has no distinctive role of his own (*precantur celebrans et populus*).

It would be out of place to engage now in further discussion of this matter, important as it undoubtedly is. The secret recitation of the *anaphora* was an unfortunate device to emphasize the august mystery of the Eucharist, but, in fact, it only obscures the common and corporate nature of the eucharistic celebration, especially in the situation when the people are not aware of the content of the prayer offered by the celebrant on their behalf. Strangely enough, it is often contended today that the congregation should not know the text of the *anaphora,* and special editions of the Euchologion are sometimes produced for the use of the worshippers, in which all secret prayers, including the *anaphora,* are simply omitted, under the pretext that they do not concern the congregation, being, as it were, a kind of private prayer of the officiating clergy. That, of course, is poor and confused theology, in flat contradiction of the open purpose and intention of the eucharistic rite itself.[13]

At present, however, we are concerned only with the liturgical function of the deacon, and are interested in the rite only insofar as it helps to clarify the nature of the diaconal assistance. There is nothing in the divine liturgy that might authorize us to regard the deacon as being more than a subordinate liturgical assistant of the officiating or celebrating priest. Certain parts of the rite are normally performed by deacons, always under the authority of the priest and in conjunction with his function, and they can be properly denoted as *ta diakonika*; but only the priest is the acting minister of all public rites in the Church.

We have noted, in the earlier part of this chapter, that, while the assistance of the deacon in the celebration of the divine liturgy was regular, traditional, and normal, it could not, and should not, be regarded as mandatory or necessary. In other words, it does not belong to the essential structure of the eucharistic rite. Nothing essential is missing in the rite when the priest celebrates alone, and this situation is formally anticipated in the rubrics of the Euchologion. Indeed, in our time Divine Liturgy is more often celebrated without the participation of the deacon than with it. Of course, in this case, the priest himself has to perform certain functions of the deacon, as, for instance, the recitation of the litanies. This may create some practical inconveniences: the priest will have to say both the litanies and his own secret prayers, which are supposed to be said simultaneously. These inconveniences, however, can be easily obviated, and moreover, the rite itself will be enriched if the priest reads aloud his own prayers before the concluding doxology. It seems that the whole rite may assume more unity and cohesion if celebrated without the deacon's assistance, so that its basic purpose and ultimate aim are better focused and enhanced. On the whole, the participation of the deacon is a matter of convenience, not of substance.

A further question now arises: does the participation of the deacon, *in its contemporary form and shape*, really serve that ultimate purpose for which the eucharistic rite is intended and instituted, or may it, in certain cases, obscure and even impede that purpose? It is a grave and crucial question, and a delicate one, so that often it is cautiously avoided. It is significant, however, that in the Russian Church, in the early years of this century, the usefulness of the diaconate, in its contemporary form, and even its necessity, were vigorously challenged by certain prominent bishops, of the conservative wing of the Russian episcopate of that time. It has been contended that it was simply useless and to no purpose to have deacons in the parish churches; that it was, rather, a meaningless custom, or just a fashion; and the hope has been expressed that the parish diaconate might go out of fashion altogether and rather soon.[14] The reasons for such radical intervention were mixed and obviously "situation conditioned." The problem was neither deeply probed, nor traced to its basic theological presuppositions. Nevertheless, this challenge, coming from competent and authoritative quarters, cannot be easily dismissed or ignored.

As a matter of fact, in the Russian Church, for various and manifold historical reasons, the diaconate has lost, in modern times, its spiritual significance and has degenerated into a kind of ceremonial or artistic office. The deacon has become practically a musical officer in the Church. His participation in the rite was sought mainly because it was expected to add to the external impressiveness of the rite, to its emotional and esthetic appeal. The main requirement of a deacon, accordingly, was to have a good and powerful voice and artistic skill; his function was divorced from the true purpose of the rite. Here it seems proper to mention one characteristic abuse which, unfortunately, has become almost a custom in many communities: deacons are often permitted to serve without preparation, that is, without the required fasting and without the intention to receive communion at the celebration in which they are taking part. It is true that, in this case, they are not supposed or allowed to function at all in the sacramental part of the divine liturgy, and their role is limited to the *enarxis*, that is, to the recitation of litanies and the reading of lessons, although the discipline on this point is often rather lax. In fact, this restriction itself only underlined the abnormality and ambiguity of the usage.[15] The deacon came to be regarded as an accidental participant in the rite, in which he was invited to perform certain functions of artistic and decorative character, without being spiritually engaged in the celebration of the mystery. Indeed, this is not only an abuse, but a characteristic abuse, reflecting the current misconception of the diaconal office. The deacon has lost his proper position in the liturgical office.

This misconception of the diaconal office is rooted to a great extent in the general overemphasis on the esthetical aspect of the divine rite which has been growing in modern times, especially in the Russian Church. The choir has assumed a disproportionate role in the rite, and the rite itself has become a sort of artistic performance. The esthetic aspect is indeed essential to the sacred rite, in which there is ample room for art. Art and esthetics, however, must be subordinate to the spiritual purpose of the rite, but they tend to run an independent and autonomous course. The modern history of music in the Russian Church is a conspicuous example of such distortion, but it would be out of place to discuss this complex subject at length at this point.[16] Only against this general background is it possible to understand properly the current shift in the character of the diaconate.

The other important factor in the process was the growing custom of infrequent communion. Whatever may be said, and is being said, in the defense of the habit of non-communicating attendance which still prevails and is often even enforced in Orthodox communities; in spite of the vigorous challenge and appeal of such a great and saintly master as Father John of Cronstadt and many others before and after him, one cannot underestimate the obvious spiritual danger inherent and implicit in this habit. It encourages the faithful to regard the Eucharist as a kind of sacred spectacle which may be attended without any deeper engagement in the very purpose of the divine rite. By its very structure, and also by the purpose of its divine institution, the eucharistic rite is inwardly ordained toward Communion, and culminates precisely in the solemn call "to draw near," addressed to the congregation. Only in this perspective can the participants in the service find their proper place. According to the authoritative interpretation of the Fathers, and of the later Byzantine commentators, the liturgy certainly is, in a sense, a "sacred panorama," a comprehensive symbolic image of the whole *oikonomia* of salvation: it requires and implies vision and contemplation. But obviously this contemplation finds its fullness only in communion. In other words, attendance finds its justification precisely in participation, which is the only real focus of attendance. The current over-emphasis on the artistic side distorts the perspective and actually impedes contemplation. In contemporary practice, the congregation, "the Holy People," in the phrase of Cabasilas, is reduced to silence, to the role of spectator; it loses its true part in the service which is, in principle and essence, precisely the corporate action of the whole Church, as gathered for celebration, in which it is at once the privilege and the bounden duty of all believers to participate. All functions in the divine rite are coordinated precisely at this point; if they are not, the inner unity of the rite may be completely lost. This is what has actually happened with the diaconal function in the contemporary situation.

It is for this reason that the question arises whether the diaconal assistance, *in its contemporary form,* is really desirable, even for the *plene esse* of the rite. At this point we are facing a dilemma. On the one hand, one may dispense altogether with the assistance of the deacon in the eucharistic rite, since this assistance in its contemporary form does not seem to serve the true and ultimate purpose of the rite. This has been done already on a large scale, if only for accidental reasons, and the venture seems to have been justified by its results. The priest is able to exercise more effectively his role as a minister of unity in his local congregation,[17] and the congregation recovers its own and proper part in the divine service. It has been not infrequently suggested that common and congregational singing be restored in order to make the participation of the people real and effective. It has been done in many communities in the Russian Church and the purpose has been achieved.

On the other hand, the existing diaconate may be reorganized and restored to its proper role of liturgical assistants of the priests in the eucharistic service. A closer liturgical relationship must be restored between the priest and his deacon on the basis of their *joint* participation in the eucharistic celebration, as it is actually anticipated in the traditional rite, although the mode of their participation will be different. The concept of liturgical assistance must be clarified and properly defined; then the participation of the deacon in the service may become an organic part of the divine rite. This prospective restoration of the true liturgical diaconate can be achieved, however, only in the context of a comprehensive liturgical renewal. Valid arguments may be adduced in favor of either alternative; they must be carefully scrutinized and pondered. This would require a theological resassessment of the whole problem of ministry. The nature of Christian ministry is always defined in the Orthodox tradition in close relation to the sacraments, especially to the holy Eucharist. The theological key to the problem of the diaconate lies in the doctrine of the Eucharist, and actually the whole problem of ministry is a eucharistic problem: the Eucharist is the heart and the center—and indeed the foundation—of the Church, which is herself the Body of Christ. The diaconate, as a distinct ministerial order, can be understood adequately only in this eucharistic setting.[18]

As a matter of fact, the permanent diaconate has survived in the Eastern Church, if in a very peculiar form. At all times there has been, in the Church a large body of deacons, both in the cathedrals and in the parishes. The composition of this group was mixed. In the Russian Church one can discern two main categories. First, there was a distinct group of those who were selected for this position on the basis of their musical ability, mainly in the cathedrals or in large city churches. They had to remain permanently in their office simply because they were selected for special reasons, as qualified precisely for the diaconal function. Many in this group had an adequate theological training and could therefore be assigned to additional duties, including preaching and catechetical instruction, if required. Second, there was a much larger group of those who had to remain deacons because they were not qualified for promotion.

This peculiar situation can be understood only in historic perspective. The instance of the Russian Church is especially significant in this respect. For various historic reasons, which cannot be discussed at length in this paper, the clergy in the Russian Church gradually became a closed and hereditary social group, a kind of a special class, or even a caste. This situation was decreed by state law and was rigorously maintained; it could not fail to foster the development of a peculiar class-consciousness, for even the families of the clergy belonged by law to "the clergy." The unity of the clergy was a social phenomenon in the total structure of a neatly stratified society. "Clergy" was a legal status, not an ecclesiastical institution. The school system, established in the eighteenth century, was the chief factor in securing the unity of the class. It was the duty of bishops to establish schools in their dioceses, and it was the legal obligation of all the clergy to send all their boys to these schools, under severe sanctions and threats of prosecution for desertion in the case they failed to do so. These were general schools, not specifically theological, and theology was taught only in two upper forms. The course was long, the curriculum dry and heavy, and discipline oppressive. Only a tiny minority of those who were compulsorily enrolled at an early age was able to graduate. Those who left the school before graduation were in constant danger of being conscripted as soldiers, or compelled to join the ranks of peasantry, unless they were given some position in the Church. This explains the disproportionate inflation of the lower ranks of the clergy in the Russian Church, and it affected the social status of the diaconate. Most deacons, especially in the rural parishes, had a very inadequate education, and could not be promoted to any higher or responsible position. Moreover, their economic situation was often alarmingly poor. This created a sharp social split within the ranks of the clergy. It is true that this system was legally abrogated about a century ago, in the era of Great Reforms in the 1860s; but its consequences were still felt quite strongly, even in the early years of this century, and inveterate habits continued. The diaconate was, in fact, a professional group in the Church rather than a vocational one. The abnormality of this situation has been sharply exposed by many bishops of the Russian Church, especially in the period of Pre-Conciliar discussions in 1904-07, and then at the Great Council of 1917-18.[19] These social conditions complicated the problem of the nature and function of the diaconate in the Russian Church. The existing permanent diaconate could not fulfill the purpose that would vindicate its existence. In other Orthodox Churches the situation was different, according to the historic and local conditions, but the basic problem was always the same. Many problems of the past are now obsolete and antiquated, especially in the Churches behind the Iron Curtain, but the memories of the past still weigh heavily on today's canonical and theological thinking.

The contemporary problem of the diaconate, as it is conceived and discussed rather intensively in the West, is more the problem of *diakonia* in a wider sense than that of the diaconate as a distinct hierarchical order. In the Eastern Churches the situation is different. In spite of the crisis and confusion outlined above, the Eastern Church is primarily concerned with the liturgical diaconate. This does not mean that the Orthodox Church is indifferent to the great and grave problem of *diakonia*, of the social responsibility and service of the Church; but it may be contended, from the Orthodox point of view, and in the light of the historic tradition of the Eastern Church, that *diakonia* in this sense cannot serve as a basis for the diaconate as an order. *Diakonia* is but a function or a task, and it is the task of the whole Church. It may be further contended that this task can be accomplished rather by the laity in the Church, under special commission from the hierarchy and under its supervision. In certain cases an ordination to minor orders may be desirable. As a matter of fact, many of the diaconal tasks, in this large sense of the word, have been for a long time successfully exercised in the Orthodox Churches by lay people: in the field of missions, of education, and religious education in particular, of charity and social service. For these tasks, from the Orthodox point of view, there is no need to restore a permanent diaconate. These tasks and duties belong to the common competence and responsibility of the whole Church. In this connection one should think rather of the restoration of the old and traditional office of the deaconesses (of which there has been constant talk in the Russian Church during the last hundred years), of the expansion of sisterhoods and especially of medical sisterhoods, and of many other similar institutions. These are indeed urgent and impending problems; but they are outside the scope of this paper.[20] Many of these tasks may be assigned to deacons, but rather on the basis of individual competence or vocation, and not as an intrinsic component of the diaconal ministry, in the proper sense.

THE ORDER OF DEACONS
IN ANGLICANISM

A SURVEY
by Richard T. Nolan

"It is evident unto all men, diligently reading Holy Scripture and ancient Authors, that from the Apostles' time there have been these Orders of Ministers in Christ's Church—Bishops, Priests, and Deacons." This statement is the opening portion of the "Preface" to the Book of Common Prayer's Ordinal, "being the Form of Making, Ordaining, and Consecrating Bishops, Priests, and Deacons" (p. 529). This threefold ministry is a basic theological principle held throughout the Anglican communion, the churches stemming from the Church of England and continuing in communion with the See of Canterbury. Though some subtle theological differences exist among Anglicans, such as the degree of necessity of this polity to the Church, there is a consensus regarding its positive contributions and desirability for a truly catholic people of God.

The order of deacons, being one of the three ordained ministries in Anglicanism, is best understood theologically through the Book of Common Prayer and, further, through Canon Law. Although national Anglican churches have slight variations in the Ordinal, all versions share the essentials of the diaconal office. Canonical regulations vary, too, not only among national churches, but also on some relatively minor points from diocese to diocese.

The Prayer Book and Canon Law in use in the Episcopal Church in the United States of America reflect the spirit and general understandings of the whole Anglican Communion's uses of the order. This is not to imply that all of the American ideas and practices can be found in every Anglican diocese, but rather, generally speaking, whatever can be found in any area of the communion is reflected somewhere in American Canon Law and the Prayer Book. Therefore, for the purpose of setting a perspective for the subsequent essays in this chapter, this survey will refer to the American versions.

Within the service for the "Ordering of Deacons," there is a public examination of the candidate; this precedes the actual laying on of hands. "The questions put to the ordinand concern: (1) his calling to the Ministry, both inwardly by the Holy Spirit and outwardly by the Church; (2) his faith in the teaching of Holy Scripture; (3) his readiness to undertake the duties of the Diaconate—liturgical, catechetical, and pastoral; and (4) his manner of life, both private and official."[1] An attempt to understand the order might be best begun by reading how the Prayer Book Examination lists the diaconal duties.

> It appertaineth to the Office of a Deacon, in the Church where he shall be appointed to serve, to assist the Priest in Divine Service, and specially when he ministereth the Holy Communion, and to help him in the distribution thereof; and to read Holy Scriptures and Homilies in the Church; and to instruct the youth in the Catechism; in the absence of the Priest to baptize infants; and to preach, if he be admitted thereto by the Bishop. And furthermore, it is his Office, where provision is so made, to search for the sick, poor, and impotent people of the Parish, that they may be relieved with the alms of the Parishoners, or others.[2]

As has been noted in one study, "The powers of this Order are distinctly limited. The Deacon may neither celebrate the Holy Communion nor pronounce God's Absolution or Benediction, though he may assist in the administration of any Sacrament."[3] Some undefined areas of diaconal prerogatives yet remain; for example, in some states a deacon may officiate at a solemnization of matrimony. Problems that arise in this case include: Can a deacon rightly use the blessing of the Prayer Book Service? Is a substitution of this blessing with another form in keeping with the rubrics? Similar problems arise with the blessings in the "Order for the Burial of the Dead." Though many of the duties are quite clearly stated in the Prayer Book, there are questions yet unanswered officially, and others can be raised, even regarding the appropriateness of certain of these duties for deacons in the contemporary Church.

The formal preparation for this ministry in the American church is spelled out in detail in Canon 34.[4] Highlights of this canon have been summarized as follows:

> To become a Deacon a man must be a baptized and confirmed communicant of the Church, at least twenty-one years of age. Before his ordination he passes through the preliminary stages of Postulant and Candidate for Holy Orders, during which time he fulfills the requirements of the Canon Law as to his studies, examination, and general preparation for the Ministry. After his ordination to the Diaconate, he normally remains in that office a year[5] before being admitted to the higher Order of Priesthood.[6]

It should be noted that there are men prepared fully for advancement to the priesthood who decide to remain Deacons (see Dr. Cherbonnier's essay). This is a sort of limbo state, so far as the Prayer Book and Canon Law now provide.

The second general use of the diaconate is set by Canon Law; this is often referred to (unsatisfactorily) as the "perpetual diaconate." Canon 34, Section 10, sets the tone for this use as follows: "A man of devout character and proved fitness, desirous to serve in the capacity of a Deacon without relinquishing his secular occupation and with no intention of seeking advancement to the Priesthood, may be accepted as a Postulant and admitted as a Candidate. . . ." Conditions placed thereon include an age requirement of not less than thirty-two years and fulfillments of modified academic requirements.[7] The practical limitations are designated in this Section:

> A Deacon ordained under the provisions of this Section shall exercise his Ministry as assistant in any parish or parishes to which, at the request or with the consent of the Rector and Vestry, he may be assigned by the Ecclesiastical Authority. As such assistant he may execute all functions appertaining to the Office of a Deacon[8]. . . . He may not be transferred to another jurisdiction except upon the express request in writing of the Ecclesiastical Authority thereof.[9]

Prior to the General Convention of 1964, the clause "he may not in any respect act as Minister in charge of a congregation" was contained in the above quoted Section. A change made in 1964 permits deacons to become ministers-in-charge of parishes and missions in the absence of rectors.[10] Thus, the so-called "perpetual diaconate" seems to be emerging as an order in its own right, distinct from the waiting period for priesthood, and utilized for specifically diaconal tasks.

At one point, however, the Prayer Book seems to support only the transitional diaconate, for in the collect before the benediction in the ordination service these words are said: ". . . that they, having always the testimony of a good conscience, and continuing ever stable and strong in the Son Christ, may so well behave themselves in this inferior Office, that they may be found worthy to be called unto the higher Ministries in thy Church. . . ."[11] This is hardly an implication or incentive for a man to remain a deacon.

Although it is not to be denied that variations on the above themes are in practice within the Anglican communion, it can be assumed that the general provisions for the order, as have been discussed above, are at least possible within the Canons and Prayer Books of the national churches. Therefore, this introductory essay, though focusing upon American sources, offers the reader a feeling for the theology and uses of the order of deacons in Anglicanism.[12]

DEACONS AS "INTERNS"
by Theodore P. Ferris

When we speak of an intern we normally refer to a young man or woman who has recently been graduated from a medical school and is now a resident member of the medical staff of a hospital. During his internship he works under the direction of experienced doctors, is in immediate contact with the patients, but does not take the full responsibility for the decisions made or the action taken. He learns how to apply the principles and theories he studied in medical school; he begins to see that to know what a principle is and to know how to practice it are two quite different things. He is a doctor, but still an intern. He makes decisions under the advisement of a more experienced man, and is relieved of the full responsibility if the decision should be wrong.

No one, most likely, would want to be under the care of a doctor who had not had this kind of training. No matter how fine a record a man might have in medical school, this period of internship is universally required of him before he begins to practice medicine on his own.

The same thing cannot be said about the preparation for the Christian ministry. In our branch of the Anglican Communion a man usually does "field work" while he is in theological studies. This means that he spends a part or all of Sunday, and sometimes Saturday as well, in a parish. He does the things a layman can do, like teaching a church school class, leading a young people's fellowship, making parish calls, and, if he has a lay reader's license, he often reads part of the service to help the rector, but chiefly to gain confidence and experience in leading public worship. The amount of time he can give to this part of his work varies, but at best it is limited, and through no fault of his own, he is not yet prepared to do much more than any other willing layman can do.

In addition to this "field work," he usually spends one or

two summers in "clinical training." During this period he has the advantage of not being divided between his academic responsibilities and his clinical work. Working under supervision in an institution which cares for those who are mentally or physically disabled, he comes in close contact with human beings, and begins to realize that the Christian Gospel, while it is given and, in a certain sense, fixed and final, must nevertheless be flexible enough to reach every conceivable variety of human ailment and need.

In most cases he is graduated from the theological school, ordained to the diaconate, and then either assumes the full responsibility of a mission or a small parish, or becomes an assistant or curate to the rector of a large parish. Whichever he does, he is virtually thrown into the rough waters of the ministry to sink or swim without much help from anyone. If he is in charge of a mission or small parish, there is no one to give the help; and if he is a curate, the rector is usually too busy to help him.

These two facts stare us in the face: there is nothing in the training of a priest comparable to the internship in the training of a doctor, and nothing is more greatly needed by priests, as well as doctors, than this period of guided work in which a man has all the authority of his profession and at the same time has someone to turn to in time of doubt, and someone to report to at the end of the day. The result of this situation can be disastrous. A man well trained in the seminary can go into a small parish and, with the best intentions in the world, can ruin it in six months. He knows the theories, but he does not know people. He does not know that his convictions and beliefs cannot be imposed upon anyone, no matter how correct they may be.

He studies canon law in the seminary but he has no opportunity there to learn how the canons can best be administered. A wise rector, for example, rarely, if ever, goes into a vestry meeting with a copy of the canons under his arm, nor does he begin a meeting of the music committee by announcing that the rector has complete authority over the music of the church. He knows that he does have such authority, but he also knows that the music committee consists of human beings, and he can best exert his authority by sharing the responsibility with them and taking them into his confidence.

Likewise he studies theology in the seminary. He learns that human nature is not so pure as people once thought it to be, that there is such a thing as original sin, and that the accent on judgment is needed to balance the accent on love. Knowing these things, however, is no assurance that the student knows how to apply this knowledge when he is face to face with an individual in trouble. One person may already be so overladen with guilt that what he needs most is the assurance of forgiveness, not judgment. Another person may be so unaware of his shortcomings that he needs his conscience awakened, and if necessary, shocked into life.

Lacking this experience in the application of what he has learned to specific situations, he makes mistakes and, because he is alone, he must take all the consequences of them. Sometimes he is never aware of the mistakes and, if he is, has no idea how to repair the damage. Nine times out of ten he resorts to his authority as a deacon or priest of the Church and thereby magnifies the mistake.

In other communions serious attempts have been made to meet this situation. Some interdenominational theological schools are willing to release a student for a year's internship in a parish. After that year he returns to the school and finishes his training. I am in no position to make any judgment on this plan inasmuch as I have not been involved in it in any way. When I first heard of it, two questions came to my mind at once. First, what will it do to a student to pluck him out of an academic atmosphere, plant him temporarily in the confusion of a busy parish, and then put him back in the cloisters of thought, meditation, and speculation? Second, how much help will such a man be to the minister of a parish who, in most cases, is not prepared to give much time to the perplexities and questions of the intern? The few ministers I happen to know who have worked with the "intern" plan confirm my doubts about it. Granted that it is better than nothing, it is, in some ways, comparable to letting a medical student practice on patients before he has finished his professional training.

The question that the Anglican communion must face is, what is the relationship between this crying need for a period of internship and the diaconate? Speaking only for the Episcopal Church in the United States, and only as I see it through my own limited vision, I would say that, at present, there is virtually no connection between the two. There are rare parishes where the deacon is, in fact, an intern. The staff is large enough so that he is not pressed into responsibilities he is not ready to assume, and the rector is not so pressed that he cannot assume the responsibility for guiding and directing the work of the deacon.

It will be admitted by most of our clergy that these instances are relatively rare. The deacon is more often like a diver on a springboard, shifting his weight, getting his balance, waiting for the moment to make the final plunge. His diaconate is a six-months' waiting period in which he sometimes impatiently longs for the time when he will be the real thing.

The basic problem of the internship is not a question of orders; it is a question of finding parishes prepared to do the training. At the present moment there are not many of them. There could be more if the bishops and the deans of seminaries insisted on this as part of a man's preparation for the ministry, and the Church made some financial provision for this undertaking. If the places could be found where this kind of training could be given, it does not seem to me that it would make much difference whether the intern were in the lesser order of the diaconate or in priest's orders. It is conceivable, however, that if the diaconate were widely recognized as a period of internship, and the deacons were not treated as premature priests, the fact that the intern had been truly "set apart" for the ministry, yet not ordained to all the privileges and obligations of the priesthood, might be the most suitable conditions under which a valuable internship could take place.

FULL–TIME PASTORAL MINISTRY
by George H. Emerson

The perpetual diaconate had long been in my contemplation. For a number of years before I made application for admission as a postulant, my own inclinations, reinforced by the urgings of my rector, had turned more and more toward this much-to-be-desired goal. My lay involvement in the work of the Church, like that of so many perpetual deacons, had become increasingly greater with the years: vestryman, junior warden, senior warden, lay reader, canvass chairman, building committee chairman, and various aspects of diocesan service. The demands and accomplishments of that work, even when hindered by the clamorings of a busy law practice and upper-echelon service club work, proved to be most satisfying. However, the diaconate, as an objective, had to remain in the realm of the theoretical, since the diocese in which I was then resident made no provision for the ordination of perpetual deacons.

When I finally closed my law offices and retired, my family and I moved to a suburban area south of San Francisco. To escape the Satanic mischief for idle hands, I sought a Church affiliation where my free time and my experience might be of help. This I quickly found in the thriving Saint Andrew's Mission, in Saratoga.

I was given the position of administrative associate, which was created for the purpose. My assignment, working with the vicar, was to take care of the various problems incidental to the temporal affairs of the mission: overseeing maintenance; coordinating purchases; handling legal problems attendant on the acquisition and operation of Church property; questions of insurance; and the usual business details arising in the day-to-

day operation of a growing church. In addition, I served as
lay reader-chaplain, conducting worship services in chapel for
our Sunday School, and later organized and trained a corp of
chaplains to take over this work when we had three sessions of
Sunday School each Sunday.

Only a few months after this move, Bishop James Pike
made known his active encouragement of those men who might
want to study for the perpetual diaconate. With the moral support of my former rector and the vicar, I quickly took advantage of this unexpected opportunity. It held out to me, in
my new-found leisure, the possibility of my ultimately being
of greater service to my Church in holy orders than I could
reasonably expect, serving as a layman.

To implement his program for the development of the perpetual diaconate within his diocese, Bishop Pike named a priest,
the Reverend John A. Luther, who was sympathetic to the plan,
to develop and present a course of study and training for the
fifteen men who formed the first formal class of postulants.
We were called together early in 1960 and our curriculum was
laid out for us. We met twice a month during the balance
of the year, through November, for lectures by various priests,
several of whom were members of the Diocesan Board of
Examining Chaplains. We were assigned a course of outside
reading paralleling the subjects of the lectures. In December
there were a dozen of us who sat for examinations. We had
a half-day written quiz on Bible content. The second day we
had written examinations on Bible exegesis, Church history,
theology, liturgics, ethics and practical theology, and canon law.
We had a third day of oral examinations in all fields. We
were told afterwards that the examinations given to us were
the same as those given to the seminary graduates. The examining chaplains were supposed to be slightly more lenient in
grading our examinations. In any event, all of this class of
twelve were successful. Eleven of the class were ordained in
Grace Cathedral, San Francisco, on Dec. 24, 1960, by the Right
Reverend James A. Pike, then bishop of California. The one

remaining member had to wait a couple of months for the passage of the six months' candidacy required by Section 10 (b) of the National Canons (Canon 34) before he could be ordained. After a breathing spell of a couple of months, our class, again under the tutelage of Mr. Luther, and with the approval of Bishop Pike, started a course of study, extending over a year or so, leading to our being licensed to preach, after passing further examinations.

The thought of the possibility of greater service to the Church, which was the motivating factor originally impelling me to seek ordination as a perpetual deacon, I held in only the most general, if not actually vague, form. The realities of my service were much broader and far-reaching than I had at first imagined.

After ordination I was immediately delegated to read the Ante-Communion at our celebrations of the Eucharist. As a matter of fact, our class was ordained on the morning of Christmas Eve and all of us then participated in Christmas Eve services in our several churches. Also, with my ordination, I rotated with the two priests in our mission, as it then still remained, in officiating at morning prayer. I regularly administer private Communion, particularly to the older members of the parish. With three priests now on the staff, I am not called on to perform baptisms, solemnize marriages, nor serve at the burial of the dead. Neither am I called upon to preach more than two or three times a year.

Our parish last year organized a mission for the diocese and, serving in rotation with the other parish clergy, I officiated at services of morning prayer until the mission called a vicar. With the other parish clergy, I regularly participate in instructing Confirmation classes and at sessions of adult schools of religion. With the other associate clergy, I am *ex officio* a member of the vestry, but without a vote, and I am clerk of the vestry and parish. I also serve as chancellor of the parish, handling all the legal problems that arise, the drafting of contracts and other necessary documents, and the correspondence that forms an integral part of such matters. The requirements here are not insignificant in a parish such as ours with an ambitious, but necessary, program of land acquisition and building. All questions relating to all phases of insurance are also a part of my responsibility. Some few months after my ordination, our mission successfully made application for admission to parish status. I took care of all the legal work necessary for incorporation as a parish and the subsequent development of the parish structure. It is my privilege to serve as a sort of unofficial chancellor of the Deanery of Santa Clara, advising various of the priests from time to time.

Not infrequently I am called upon to counsel members of the parish, and even members of other parishes and missions of the deanery when their problems are law-related. I must confess that, in many instances, I find my function here little different from the counseling I offered my clients during my thirty-two years of active law practice. Strange as it may seem to those prejudiced few who look upon practitioners of the law with jaundiced eye, I find that my legal experience is of great value as I counsel with our parishioners and those from other deanery churches.

I think it safe to say that a large part of my substantially full-time service arises out of my years of practice in civil law, and the practical and varied business experience and insight which every lawyer must absorb if he is to represent his clients adequately.

As to my acceptance by the laity, I find a divergence of view. Among not a few of those who have been Episcopalians for many years, particularly those who were members of the parish before I was ordained, I would seem to inhabit a kind of ecclesiastical half-world, no longer lay, but not quite wholly clerical. Those who are younger, either chronologically or in their Church affiliation, seem to be able to accept me as one of the clergy—albeit of a substratum that is somewhat mystifying to them, and one which is most difficult for them to comprehend.

From my observation, there appear to be some few obstacles of greater or lesser degree, to the full effectiveness of the ministry of the diaconate. This is particularly true for those persons who, as long-time Episcopalians, are so familiar with our forms of service as to recognize the departures from the norms of usage which those diaconal impediments require. The difficulties in point are necessarily inherent in the office of deacon, through restrictions imposed upon, or privileges withheld from, him at his ordination.

The fact that at morning or evening prayer the deacon must use a substitute for the absolution, or nothing at all, and must use the minor benediction, does not appear to me to be too formidable. However, when a priest is present and prefers to pronounce the absolution and to dismiss the congregation with the major benediction, there may be to some in the congregation an appearance of cumbrousness. Again, I should not consider this as other than minor. Of greater significance, however, is the administration of private Communion from reserved sacraments. There the forms of service which the deacon is allowed to use are necessarily so widely divergent from the familiar forms of the Prayer Book as, quite possibly, to make such services objectionable to one who, through ready familiarity with the accustomed forms, finds the substituted forms of service something less than acceptable. While this additional point to me is wholly theoretical, since I have no occasion there to function, the requirement in this diocese that the deacon substitute a different form for the priestly blessing in the services of baptism, marriage, and burial is, to some, an obstacle to their functioning.

These problems I enumerate without any attempt to advance a solution, since any practical remedy would result in the elimination of the distinctions between the functioning of the deacon and the priest in the conduct of our services. We would then be left without any diaconate. It is certainly to be preferred that the diaconate function with its slight handicaps than not to function at all.

My relations with my rector are of the best. He gives me his complete support, encouragement, and endorsement. He is heartily in favor of the concept of the perpetual diaconate, both in the abstract and the concrete. He is as enthusiastically convinced of the merits of the services rendered by the perpetual deacons as are the deacons themselves. My rector freely makes use of such of my services and talents as to him appear of value, probably to the maximum permissible canonically. It must be admitted, however, that I sometimes have to call upon all the humility of which I am capable as I am required to take a position subordinate to a young curate, recently out of the seminary. However intelligent, able, and energetic he may be, he is lacking in experience and, incidentally, had not yet been born at a time when I was already established as a successful lawyer. That exercise in humility, however, is good practice, and it helps to maintain one's sense of proportion more nearly in balance, and to keep one's ego properly deflated.

My contacts with our ordinary and our suffragan have been most satisfactory, indeed gratifying. Each of them has shown me the utmost consideration and graciousness. I am not alone in this experience and reaction. From my conversations with the two dozen or so other perpetual deacons, it is made abundantly clear that they all feel the same. Bishop Pike has appointed me to four diocesan positions: to the chancery, the marriage committee of the chancery, the convention committee on canons, and the division of voluntary ministry.*

As a part of the development of the perpetual diaconate in this diocese, it has been very carefully spelled out for us in writing what we may not and what we may do and, as to the latter, how. This clarification of what, otherwise, could well be a shadowy and troublesome area is of obvious benefit.

It is to be recognized that opinions among the priests of

---

* Editor's Note: By virtue of amendment of the diocesan canon and election by diocesan convention upon the nomination of Bishop Pike, the Ven. George H. Emerson has added to his ministry the responsibilities of Archdeacon of California.

the diocese as to the value of the perpetual diaconate are rather definitely divided. While some have not made up their minds one way or the other, most of the priests are either opposed to the whole concept, in varying degrees of opposition, or they favor the idea, again with some gradation of approval. Those priests who have perpetual deacons assisting them are among those more earnestly in favor of this aspect of the third order of clergy. It may be argued, as with the hen or the egg, whether these latter priests favor the diaconate because they have deacons assigned to them, or whether they have deacons assigned to them because they are favorably inclined to such assistance. It appears more reasonable, however, to conclude that the latter premise is the more logical, since, if a priest were opposed to the perpetual diaconate, he would hardly take the affirmative action required of him in the first instance to launch on his way the applicant for postulancy.

It has been a source of considerable gratification to me (I pray, unselfishly) that I have, with my ordination, been able to devote my energies more deeply and, I hope, more effectively, in the work of our Savior than in the past in my lay capacity. Then, too, my additional study, both before and since my ordination, has broadened my knowledge and understanding, and has given me a greater appreciation of the depth and significance of the teachings of Jesus Christ; and in recognition of the overwhelming exploration still to be made, it spurs me on to further study in the search for even fuller insight.

What, then, is my message to those laymen who have been engaged in Church work over the years? We are faced constantly with the crying need for more clergy to serve the Church. How better to help meet that need than to do it yourself! Predicated upon my own experience, where my legal training has proved to be of such benefit when coupled with my service in holy orders, I would postulate as a general rule the statement that any man's experience gained in earning a living would stand his Church in good stead when taken in combination with his work as a perpetual deacon. I would not limit this to the so-called learned professions: to the lawyer, doctor, engineer, architect, accountant, and teacher. Any executive, administrator, salesman, musician, social service worker, a member of any of the skilled trades, and so on *ad infinitum*, would find his secular experience called into play in the most unexpected ways as a part of his service in the diaconate. Such services are rendered to the Church at no expense, a saving to his Church as against its having to call on one earning his living in such a calling and, in most instances, with a degree of interest and of concern seldom found in one not in close relationship to his Church.

Even in our own thriving parish the fact that the services of a perpetual deacon are available substantially full time makes possible activities and practices to a greater depth and detail than would be possible were those services not there, except at a considerably greater burden on the three priests now serving. This is not a unique situation. It is a matter of simple arithmetic equally applicable in any parish.

All of the two dozen perpetual deacons in the diocese are serving actively, to the extent that their free time permits, although the others are not so fortunate as I in being able to devote full time. Our activities are manifold, varying from parish to parish as different needs are met, but serving we all are, well, truly, and happily, and to the relief and even joy of the priests with whom we are associated, and without monetary compensation. We all feel that the joy of service is adequate recompense for what we so gladly offer.

The potentialities for the services of perpetual deacons are infinite. In a parish or mission where the load is too great for one priest, but where the financial burden attendant upon the calling of a second priest is too much to assume, a perpetual deacon is the obvious answer.

If there be need for the establishment of a new mission in an area not adequately served by an existing parish or mission, but where, because of financial limitation, the expense of a vicar is, for the moment, out of the question, a perpetual deacon can be assigned to that mission at its organization to serve until its finances improve to the point where it can support all or the necessary major part of a vicar's compensation.

Again an existing mission may, for a variety of reasons, find itself in financial difficulty, and the diocese, because of other commitments, might be unable to assume the expense of the vicar's compensation. Rather than close the mission, the diocese could move the vicar to another location where he was needed and assign a perpetual deacon to the mission until its prospects brighten.

These examples are patently not intended to be all-inclusive. They are but parts of a theme, the variations of which are infinite.

As to the value of, and the need for, the services of perpetual deacons, I am, admittedly, not without prejudice and something less than wholly objective. I feel impelled to say, somewhat categorically, that the experience in the diocese of California, under the guidance of our bishop, has proved conclusively that the need for a substantial perpetual diaconate is a great and continuing one. It is, indeed, a need which cannot readily be met, whether in California or any other diocese in our Church, in any other way except at a burdensome, if not insuperable, cost.

A DEACON'S "RAISON d'ETRE"
by Edmond LaB. Cherbonnier

Some years ago, following a church service in which I had taken part, the rector's wife was heard to remark, "To look at that young man, you would never suspect that he could not qualify for the priesthood." This essay provides me, at long last, with an opportunity to reply, and to explain why one might remain a deacon, not from incompetence, but by choice.

Historically, of course, the diaconate needs neither justification nor apology. It was once a recognized order of the ministry, with distinct functions of its own. To this day, in some branches of Christendom, the deacon still retains his separate identity. In the Episcopal Church, however, the diaconate has atrophied. The Prayer Book itself is partly responsible. In the service for the ordering of deacons, one of the prayers expresses the hope that they "may so well behave themselves in this inferior office, that they may be worthy to be called unto the higher ministries (p. 535)." Small wonder that the diaconate is regarded as merely a stepping stone to the priesthood, an apprenticeship to be discharged as quickly as possible.

My own reasons for remaining a deacon, however, would probably not satisfy the stickler for canon law. They are based, less upon historical grounds, than upon contemporary circumstances. They are similar to the reasons which have prompted churchmen like Bishop Robinson to call for a radical re-thinking of traditional Christian belief and practice. Most of these arguments point, in one way or another, to one insistent fact: the ministry, as presently conceived, has lost its effectiveness. This is most obviously true in the vast urban areas, where Christian influence has dwindled to insignificance. It is less obvious, but equally true, in the suburbs, where church membership is impressive, but where a veneer of Christian forms and symbols conceals an underlying culture-religion which is often indistinguishable from paganism.

Consider first the Church's abdication from the modern metropolis. A dramatic example is the parish of Woolwich, in Bishop Robinson's own diocese. It is a run-down parish in a depressed area of greater London, with a total of 12,000 people. For the past five years a blue ribbon team of four dynamic young clergymen have labored night and day to breathe life into the remains of this once flourishing congregation. Their accomplishments are summarized, in the following words, by the rector:

> We have tried to pray and to love. We have tried to be humble and sensitive. We have played every card in the pack . . . We have done everything we set out to do. We have raised a

fortune and spent it. But we have achieved virtually none of the modest things we had hoped for. If each priest on our staff had persuaded ten people each year to join the church, we should have had a congregation of 400. Yet the regular members of the congregation have increased from about fifty to 100, mostly from socially superior areas outside our working-class parish. We have quite obviously failed.[13]

Here is proof positive that the priesthood, as currently conceived, can no longer make contact with the realities of the twentieth century. No one can say that the four priests failed for lack of talent, or dedication, or effort, or training, or money. They failed, either because Christianity itself is passé, or because the ministry in its present form does not mediate the Gospel. Those who deny the latter explanation must be prepared to accept the former.

In the suburban churches, the picture is quite different, at least on the surface. Church membership is at an all-time high, at least in the United States; "religion" is becoming an increasingly popular subject in colleges and universities, in magazines and moving pictures, and even at cocktail parties; and even the perennial shortage of clergy has become less acute. Nevertheless, the upsurge of interest in "religion" does not necessarily mean a revival of Christianity. It could, in fact, spell the opposite. For the real danger to Christianity has never been atheism, but some rival religion, and the threat is most deadly when the rival masquerades in Christian garb.

Today's impostor has been unmasked by a self-critical group of Christian sociologists. Gibson Winter, for example, documents the evidence in *The Suburban Captivity of the Churches*. Peter Berger does the same in *The Noise of Solemn Assemblies*. The suburban church, they point out, is not so much a place where consciences are pricked as it is a forum for self-congratulation; less a medium of divine judgment than a mirror for magnifying middle-class values; less a source of renewal than an outlet for romantic sentiment.

All this is scarcely the fault of the individual clergyman.

He is rather the victim of the system. He often has a clear idea of what he would like to accomplish, but is prevented by the public image which society fastens upon him. His time and energy are preempted by an endless round of administrative detail, trivial meetings, and ceremonial appearances. Most frustrating of all, the words he uses do not seem to get through. People imagine that they know in advance whatever a clergyman might have to say. If he does not actually say it, they attribute this to inarticulateness on his part. The cutting edge of the Gospel is blunted by the mass of religious clichés with which the modern mind is stuffed. No wonder that, as numerous surveys have shown, a startling number of parish clergy would leave their posts if they could. Their discontent does not betray a lack of faith, but rather the opposite. They are thwarted by subtle pressures which prevent them from putting their faith into practice.

Like a twentieth-century monarch, the priest is the prisoner of society's expectations. Like the monarch, he too has been progressively shorn of his powers. He was once the best educated man in town; today his educational advantage is often hard to detect. He was once an arbiter of manners; today he is a favorite subject of caricature. His was once a vocation for sons of the nobility; today he must often overcome parental opposition. He was once a prize catch for the town belle; today the wife of an English vicar has written a warning to all eligible young ladies never to marry a minister. His plight has been described by O. Hobart Mowrer, the psychologist:

> Politicians, union and management executives, scientists are the *real* prophets today. Social workers and public agencies *really* deal with the poor, hungry, sick, jailed, orphaned, prostitutes, elderly and delinquent. The psychoanalyst, psychiatrist and clinical psychologist *really* help troubled, neurotic, guilty lost souls. Unions and secular civil rights groups engage in *real* social action. . . . No wonder we have trouble recruiting for the ministry![14]

No single reason can be given for this state of affairs. It is the cumulative result of a series of causes historical, sociological, and theological. The theological cause is the one which I want especially to single out, for it is the one which the Church, particularly through its deacons, can most readily overcome. I refer to the psychological chasm which now exists between clergy and laity. That such a chasm exists at all is often stoutly and sincerely denied by a great many priests. But it is not denied by the layman. It can be demonstrated by a simple experiment. Let a clergyman in civilian dress be introduced to a stranger as "Mr. Parker." Then, after half an hour or so, let it be known that Mr. Parker is a clergyman. The change in the stranger's demeanor will speak for itself. He will become shy and self-conscious, wondering whether he has said anything to offend. Or he may feel called upon to demonstrate his moral earnestness or spiritual sensitivity. More refreshingly, he may go out of his way to show how profane and cynical he can be. The one thing he will hardly ever do is to remain the same. The priestly presence makes him ill at ease, it puts him on the defensive.

The principal cause of this estrangement is theological. The Church's teaching has often suggested that the priest lives on a higher plane than other mortals. A recent article in a Roman Catholic magazine says this explicitly. The priest, it insists, is raised above the mundane sphere of time and multiplicity to the loftier realm of eternity, unity, and truth. The layman, belonging to the lower realm, "has not the charism of clear discernment. . . . He does not clearly see; he can, so to speak, only hear and act."[15] In effect, this means that the clergy give the orders and the laity carry them out. Nor may the priest step down from Olympus to share the laymen's burden or to take responsibility for the fate of the world. The priest who does so "violates his own vocation, laicizes himself in his heart, and ultimately, because of this corruption of values, becomes thoroughly committed to the temporal sphere."[16]

Such a relation between clergy and laity is hardly biblical.

In fact, the Bible rejects the natural tendency of so many religions to invest the priesthood with a mystique. The Bible recognizes differences of function, but not of caste, for God is no respecter of persons.

The present chasm between clergy and laity is rather a corruption of biblical teaching. Though its causes are complex, the clergy did at least acquiesce in being put on a pedestal. In so doing, they brought about their own eventual demise. For a pedestal makes a poor base of operations. As medieval womanhood discovered, to be worshipped from afar is to be dependent upon the whim of the worshipper. When the layman finally tired of being a second-class Christian, the priest was by-passed, the object of public praise but private indifference. Having consented to play the role of a man apart, he now finds himself performing to an empty house.

In these circumstances, the deacon may have a special role to play. He is often in a better position than the priest to break out of this ecclesiastical quarantine. Belonging to a less exalted order, he is less conspicuously tarred with the sacerdotal brush, under less constraint to speak for the ecclesiastical establishment (or the entrenchment, as it has been called). The Roman Catholic Church has tacitly admitted as much by agreeing to discuss the possibility of permitting deacons to marry. The proposal itself acknowledges that the deacon has not completely lost his amateur standing. With one foot in the church and the other in the world, he may help to draw both closer together.

Exactly how he does this is a matter for creative experiment. One novel proposal has been made by the rector of Woolwich, with the blessing of his bishop: namely, that the minister would be taken more seriously if he earned his living at a secular job. In the present day, everybody works. Even the millionaire spends the day at his office. Earning a livelihood is part of being human. Yet the minister is an exception, or appears to be. Even though, in fact, he is on call twenty-four hours a day, on a job that requires extraordinary dedication and versatility, he is, in the eyes of many people, a parasite. He appears to work at no gainful occupation, and to live off the charity of his congregation. As a result, he is often held in disrespect, as an incompetent who cannot cope with the real world, or he is looked upon as one who stands aloof, who does not share in the common human lot, and who is, therefore, unqualified to deal with the issues of everyday life.

In biblical times it was not so. There was a strong rabbinical tradition, inherited by the early Christians, that the spiritual leader of a community should earn his living at a regular trade. Christ himself was a carpenter, St. Peter a fisherman, and St. Paul a tent maker. With St. Paul it was a matter of pride to pay his own way from city to city by plying his trade.

Before admitting defeat, the rector of Woolwich proposes to apply this apostolic example to his own Church. He plans to appoint a lay bursar to administer the parish, so that the clergy can earn their own living at secular jobs. They will, of course, have far less time to devote to strictly "religious" matters. By identifying themselves with the common lot of all men, however, they may achieve more than they did as full-time parish organizers. The results will be significant for the whole Church.

Nor is it just in impoverished parishes like Woolwich that the minister is handicapped by not supporting himself. His economic dependence is even more of a handicap in the "captive" suburban church, particularly in the discharge of his prophetic function. He can hardly call a spade a spade if, as has been charged, he is the spiritual errand boy of the rich.

In the Middle Ages the post of rector or vicar often carried with it an independent income; this is so even today in parts of England. While this undoubtedly was a temptation to slothfulness and to social conservatism, it did free the rector from the purse-strings of his flock. He could speak the unpopular truth without fear of a cut in salary. The minister of today, by contrast, must reckon with reprisals from vested interests. His position is more like that of chaplain to a medieval nobleman, whose position was secure so long as he confined himself to "spiritual" matters and did not presume to comment upon the master's private or public affairs.

One thinks, immediately, of the race question, and of the anguish of sincere ministers who must reckon with sub-Christian attitudes among their congregations. Those who take a stand are hounded out of their churches. Others muffle their indignation because of economic responsibilities to their families. In neither case is the word of God proclaimed as it could be if the clergyman were economically independent. As Harvey Cox has recently written:

> The only way in which the clergy can ever change the way in which the word they use is perceived is to refuse to play the role of antiquarian and medicine man in which society casts them, but this is difficult, because it is what they are paid for.[17]

It is hardly possible (even if it were desirable) to return to medieval practice, but it is quite possible to return to that of the earliest Christians, where the minister's economic independence preserved him from spiritual captivity. Protected against economic reprisals, he was free to declare the word of God against the *status quo*. Perhaps that explains why St. Paul could write so frankly to the Corinthians, and also why they took his words to heart: he owed them not a cent.

The rector of Woolwich intends his suggestion for priests as well as deacons. For most priests today, however, secular employment is scarcely a live option. Even if they were willing and qualified, their congregations would object. There are exceptions: the Reverend John C. Danforth, for example, spends the weekdays at his St. Louis law firm, and the weekends with his congregation. To the majority of Christians, however, the thought of a priest of the Church living by the sweat of his brow remains incongruous, if not abhorrent.

For the deacon, however, the obstacles are not so great.

His "non-commissioned" rank enables him to hold a secular job without causing so many raised eyebrows. By immersing himself in the real problems of real people, he may help to heal the breach between the Church and the world. Sitting more loosely to vested ecclesiastical interests, he may help the Church to rejoin the human race, and so to recover its original mission.

Not many have chosen this vocation. Perhaps not many should. But it is a plausible approach to one of Christianity's most pressing problems: the problem of reuniting minister and layman—whom God would join together, but whom man has put asunder. When this problem has been overcome, then this particular deacon will have lost his *raison d'être*.

ARNOLD H. LEGG

THE DIACONATE
IN THE CHURCH
OF SOUTH INDIA

I. THE BACKGROUND

(a) To approach intelligently the question of the diaconate
in the Church of South India a brief reference is necessary to
the very varied types of ministry inherited by the united Church
when it was inaugurated in 1947. Into the union came streams
from the Anglican, Congregational, Presbyterian and British
Methodist traditions, together with a smaller group associated
with the Basel Evangelical Mission, itself a union of Lutheran
and Reformed elements. It was only in the Anglican tradition,
forming rather less than half of the united Church, that there
were ordained deacons, though in the small Basel Mission section there were a few "consecrated evangelists." As these had
been consecrated with the laying on of hands, though not by
a bishop, with prayer to the Holy Spirit, for work comparable
to that of deacons, the Synod Executive Committee a few
months after the union authorized their recognition and com-
missioning as deacons. But at its inauguration, the united
Church had within it also large numbers of Congregational lay
deacons, Methodist class leaders and local preachers, and some
Presbyterian "elders." There were also Methodist "probationers"
who, like the Anglican but unlike the Congregational deacons,

were theologically trained, paid workers on the way to the full ordained ministry. In addition, there were a few Anglican and Methodist deaconesses, and in some of the other sections a few "Church sisters."

It is perhaps worth emphasizing that not only the Presbyterian elders, but also the Congregational deacons were charged by church rules with the spiritual overseeing of the congregation as well as with its financial and other business. The deacons were laymen elected by a congregation for a term of years; together with the pastor, they formed the church committee. Collectively they were responsible for putting forward candidates for baptism and communicant membership, making recommendations for church discipline and resolving disputes in the congregation. In public worship they commonly received the people's offerings and helped in the administration of the elements in the communion service. Individually the deacons were often active in Sunday school work, in evangelistic bands, and as lay preachers. In a properly organized congregation each deacon had a responsibility to keep in touch with the members resident in a particular area and lead cottage prayer meetings.

(b) Another important factor in the background was that all the Churches that came into the union employed large staffs of unordained church workers. Some, commonly called catechists or evangelists, were full-time workers, and many of these had received some theological training, varying in length from a few months to three years. Others, called teacher-catechists, were teachers in church or mission day-schools who, out of school hours, cared for the local congregation and led its services.

These unordained church workers far exceeded the ordained ministers in number and most village congregations depended more upon such local workers than upon the ordained ministry for pastoral oversight. An ordained minister might have oversight of anything from half-a-dozen to forty or fifty village groups extending over a wide area, and could only rarely visit them. This, of course, was a relatively cheap method of pastoral oversight. The teacher-catechist, if employed in a government-aided school, received the greater part of his salary from the government grant. The full-time catechists and evangelists were of lower educational standard than that required for the ordained ministry, and were paid considerably less. But this pattern of unordained ministry had developed not only, perhaps not chiefly, because of its relative cheapness. It was due also to the high regard in which the ordained ministry was held and the relatively high standards of general and theological education regarded as necessary for ordination. The supply of men who measured up to the standard was never adequate to the pastoral needs of the Church. On the whole, the Anglicans tended to accept lower academic standards for ordination, and to supplement the ordained ministry by teacher-catechists. Those of the Free Church traditions, on the whole, tended to insist that the standard of the ordained ministry must not be lowered, and to supplement their fewer ordained ministers by larger numbers of full-time catechists and evangelists with some theological training. But all these types of ministry were used by all the traditions.

(c) Except for an understanding that the existing Methodist probationers would have the same standing as Anglican deacons as regards eligibility for ordination as presbyters, no serious attempt was made before the union to reconcile these various forms of lay ministry, or in particular to reconcile the Anglican and Congregational forms of the diaconate.

There were several reasons for this. One was the deliberate policy of the negotiators to agree on matters considered essential for union, and to leave other differences to be settled by the united Church in the process of living together after union.

Another reason was that the Anglicans themselves did not seem to be very sure of the value of their ordained diaconate in its existing form. It had come to be little more than a formal stepping-stone to the priesthood, which usually followed about a year later. On the other hand, those of the Free Church traditions, who were accepting bishops for the first time, were reluctant to accept yet another unaccustomed order of the ordained ministry, especially as the Anglicans did not seem able to make out a very convincing case for it. Especially in the Congregational tradition (and this formed the larger part of one of the three negotiating churches), the office of deacon as understood therein was held in great regard, and election to it carried great prestige. Any suggestion that these deacons should be known only as "Church committee members," and their honored designation confined to young men entering the ordained ministry, was quite unacceptable.

II. THE CONSTITUTION OF THE CHURCH OF SOUTH INDIA

In the constitution, drawn up before the union and so far not amended in the relevant sections, the ordained diaconate is accorded three rules only in the chapters dealing with the ordained ministry of the Church. All forms of the lay ministry, paid and voluntary, are dealt with in a chapter headed "The Ministry of the Laity." There the legitimate and necessary functions of dedicated lay people in various types of service are fully recognized, though they are not clearly defined or distinguished. They are dealt with more exactly in the separate constitutions of the various dioceses in which they continue to serve in large numbers. They need not concern us further in this article, which is limited to the diaconate as an order of the ordained ministry.

In passing, it may be remarked that the deaconesses were absorbed in a women's order of sisters of the Church of South India, formed in 1952. The sisters are "commissioned" by the bishop without the laying on of hands, and they are not regarded as an order of the ordained ministry.

The three rules in the constitution dealing with the ordained diaconate are as follows:

> The functions of deacons shall in the Church of South India include the following—assisting the presbyter in the administration of the Lord's Supper and in other services of the Church; administering of baptism; ministering in the temporalities of the Church; giving succour to the poor, the needy and the sick; instructing of children and catechumens in the faith; preaching the Word; and generally giving assistance in pastoral and evangelistic work.
>
> The ministry of the diaconate may be undertaken for life by persons who have been accepted for this ministry by the diocesan authorities and have received due training. Persons who have been selected as candidates for the presbyterate shall ordinarily, after undergoing the necessary theological course, receive ordination to the diaconate, and undertake the duties outlined above as part of their training for the presbyterate.
>
> Deacons shall be set apart for their ministry by the laying on of hands by the bishop of the diocese. No person shall be ordained deacon until he has attained the age of twenty-three years.

These rules obviously provided for the continuance after union of the existing Anglican form of the diaconate, but the opening sentence of the second rule reveals the desire of those who negotiated the union to make the diaconate a more distinctive and significant order of the ministry. The word "ordinarily" in the next sentence has been held to justify fairly numerous exceptions to the practice of making the diaconate a necessary stepping-stone to the presbyterate. In fact, there are two dioceses out of the fifteen (both almost entirely from the Congregational tradition) which, until now, have regularly ordained men directly to the presbyterate. This is perhaps pressing the word "ordinarily" too far, but until the Church as a whole has made up its mind what it wants to make of the ordained diaconate, it is difficult to insist upon universal conformity to the present unsatisfactory form.

III. DISCUSSIONS SINCE THE UNION

The desire to make the diaconate a more distinctive and significant order of the ministry very quickly found expression. The
first synod of the united Church in 1948 asked its ministerial
committee to examine the question of the diaconate, and also
appointed a special committee to consider "Lay Deacons, Deaconesses, Readers, and other Church Workers." It was soon
found that behind both matters lay the larger question of the
nature of the diaconate in the Church of South India, and after
a while an enlarged committee was formed to consider "Deacons, Ordained and Lay." Its report, presented to the Synod of
1952 and passed on to the dioceses for study and report,
included *inter alia* the following recommendations:

1) While men to be ordained as presbyters should normally serve for a period as deacons, the diaconate should increasingly consist of men who have accepted this as a permanent calling; 2) the diaconate should include not only men for
whom this ministry is a full-time service, but also those called
to undertake it while continuing to earn their living by other
occupations; 3) there should be at least one ordained deacon in each congregation; 4) men to be ordained as deacons
should have been given some training and be not less than
thirty-five years of age; and 5) the committee of the pastorate
to which the man belongs must recommend his ordination, and
in the case of those who will exercise a permanent unpaid ministry in a particular congregation, that congregation also must
recommend the ordination.

In 1953 the executive committee of the Synod received
a long statement from the committee which reported that the
question "What is a deacon?" had become subordinated in
the discussions to another question which seemed more urgent,
namely, "How shall we provide the ministry of the Word and
Sacraments to all our village congregations?" It is wrong for
pastoral care to depend so largely on such external sources as
mission subsidies and government grants, and in any case both

are precarious. It is impossible to prosecute evangelistic work as we should if every new congregation has to have a paid worker. The system by which most village congregations receive their regular pastoral care from an unordained worker, with only rare visits for the sacraments from a minister who is almost a stranger, is destructive of the spiritual and ecclesiastical entity of the congregation as "the fellowship in one place centered on Word and Sacraments." The early Church spread by the work of volunteers, not by that of agents paid from Jerusalem or Antioch or by government grants. When the apostles had brought new congregations into being they left them in charge of a local ministry upon whom they "laid their hands." The statement recommended the development of a local presbyterate, of men given some training but continuing to get their living by other occupations. As regards the diaconate, the 1952 recommendations referred to above were reaffirmed.

But it is one thing for synod committees to make reports and recommendations; it is another matter to get them implemented in the dioceses. Such thinking seeps down only slowly and partially to diocesan and still more so to congregational level. The average Indian Christian is at least as conservative in his ways as most. Besides, there are real difficulties in finding suitable men, acceptable both to diocesan authorities and to particular village congregations, and also in securing a minimum degree of training. Teachers and farmers may be brought to a center for repeated short courses during school holidays, or periods when agricultural work is slack. But for men in other occupations it is not so easy. By the 1956 Synod, the ministerial committee was able to report that one diocese had ordained two men as honorary deacons. In another diocese two men had been recommended to the diocesan committee for this. Of these four, however, one was a retired medical officer, one a college professor, one a middle-school headmaster, and one a high school teacher—all townsmen, not villagers, serving presumably in urban rather than in village churches. The Synod ministerial committee put forward tentative rules regarding qualifications, training, etc., respectively, for honorary urban ministers, who, while living in their own homes, might help from time to time in various churches within the town or city area, and of whom a fairly good general education should be expected; and for honorary rural ministers, who would be members of the village community and tied to service in their home village where their daily occupation was, and for whom a lower standard of education might be deemed adequate. It was suggested that the authorization given by the bishop to an honorary minister should strictly limit the sphere in which he might serve.

As long ago as 1954 the Synod had asked its theological commission to study the nature of the diaconate and its functions in consultation with the parent Churches of the Church of South India, and the Faith and Order Department of the World Council of Churches. The Faith and Order Department was not at that time able to include this subject in its program of study, and although several Western scholars sent us brief essays on the diaconate in the early Church, these did not throw much light on our problems. The theological commission was also at that time preoccupied with other matters, especially the series of theological discussions between representatives of the Church of South India and the various Lutheran Churches in India, and the matter was not pursued. In 1961, however, the theological commission took up the matter again, and prepared a statement setting out the points requiring further study. This was sent by the Synod of 1962 to the dioceses for study. After considering the replies, and also a paper on "The Problem of the Diaconate," by Dr. Lukas Vischer of the World Council of Churches, the theological commission drew up a statement in 1963, for presentation to the Synod. This may be quoted almost in full.

> Some dioceses appreciated the need for reconsideration of the diaconate; others were for maintaining the *status quo*. We for our part are more than ever convinced that it is not enough to maintain the *status quo*. The diaconate as we now

have it is virtually a stepping stone to the presbyterate, and so a ministry in which a man stays for as short a time as possible. It is an inferior office with no distinctive or satisfying functions. We in the C. S. I. have a part in the effort which is going on in so many parts of the world-wide Church to re-interpret the diaconate so that it will become both more scriptural and more relevant to present needs. The C. S. I. has the advantage of being comparatively free from age-long traditions. . . . It was on the initiative of the C. S. I. that the Faith and Order Commission of the World Council of Churches has planned a study of the diaconate. Many scholars whose guidance we have sought on the question have expressed their hope that the C. S. I. would give a creative lead. . . .

The ministry, we read in Ephesians 4, was the gift to the Church of the risen and ascended Lord "for the equipment of the saints for the work of ministry, for building up the body of Christ." Through the Church, his body, Christ wills to continue and fulfill what he did when he was on earth. When we examine the activity of the incarnate Lord we find it to be a unity made up of three distinct though not mutually exclusive strands. First, he proclaimed the good news of the kingdom and sent out his disciples to make the same proclamation. Second, as the good Shepherd, he gathered together his flock and appointed his disciples to be his under-shepherds. Third, he healed the sick, cast out demons, fed the hungry, raised the dead, and these works of his compassion were signs of the present power of the kingdom which he proclaimed. If the Church is the body of Christ it should have the limbs through which the living Christ can continue the fulness of his redeeming work. It is our firm conviction that the three-fold ministry as we have inherited it is inadequate for the fulness of the work of Christ. We have means to proclaim the gospel and gather and shepherd the flock. But the present form of the diaconate does little to express and propagate the work of Christ's compassion through his Church. Though the Church has a variety of programmes of compassionate service, they are not related to the liturgical or ordained ministry of the Church.

We need to be clear that ministry in all its forms is the

ministry of the whole Church. Every member of the Church is
a part of God's chosen race, God's royal priesthood, God's
holy nation, God's own people. It is through the whole body
that the Lord continues to proclaim the word, gather the flock,
do his work of compassion. Every Christian has a part in all
these activities. In a real sense the Christian's initiation into
the Church, his baptism and confirmation, is his ordination as
God's minister, to work for Christ in the world. But it is
God's way to set aside certain called and chosen ones as special
ministers for the sake of the ministry of all—as bishops,
presbyters, and deacons. Every Christian is, in one sense, all
three partaking in the obligation to witness, love, and serve.
But some from the whole number are set aside by ordination
to be the explicit and representative organs of the Church's
whole activity in the name of Christ. The distinctive character and function of the ordained ministry is also to be
understood in terms of the liturgy (*leitourgia*), where the
Church offers her own life and the world to God, remember-
ing the sacrifice of Christ and participating in the sacrifice.
. . . The ordained ministers, therefore, have a special function
in the liturgy and help to interpret the ministry of the people
of God in the world as the ministry of Christ. Within the
three-fold ministry some who have a calling for compassionate
service are to be set aside by deacons' ordination to be the
representative organ of the Church's *diakonia* in the name
of Christ. We believe this to be a life-time calling to serve,
and that only when the diaconate is so conceived will it be a
worthy instrument of Christ's *diakonia* and a part of his total
ministry. The deacon's particular responsibility in worship
would be for the offerings of the people and the intercession
for the world. His responsibility in the world would be the
organisation, co-ordination and promotion of Christian service
and social action, a ministry which expresses Christ's compassion for his people.

The Church is called, we believe, to a new effort to
thought, prayer, and action in this matter. The first step
should be to encourage the abolition of the present stepping-
stone diaconate and ordain men direct to the presbyterate
after a period of probation. Then dioceses who wish to do so

should be permitted to take action along these lines in the selection of suitable men for the diaconate, the provision of special training and the arrangement of suitable employment for them.

In accepting this report of the theological commission, the Synod of 1964 asked dioceses to make a further study of ways in which the diaconate can be made a more meaningful ministry in the light of the fullness of the ministry of Christ along the lines indicated in the above statement, and also resolved that dioceses be encouraged to develop a pattern of diaconate which will help those called to it to accept it as a satisfying life-time ministry. But a specific recommendation that "the practice of ordaining direct to the presbyterate be recognized as *normal*, while permitting the dioceses wanting to do so to use the deacon's ordination as a preliminary to presbyteral ordination," was rejected. This would have reversed the emphasis in the present rule that candidates for the presbyterate *shall ordinarily* receive ordination to the diaconate and undertake its duties as part of their training for the presbyterate. In 1966, however, the Synod referred to the consideration of dioceses the slightly less dramatic proposal that, in order to make the transition from the present diaconate to a more meaningful diaconate possible, steps be taken to amend the Constitution by substituting *may* for *shall ordinarily*.

IV. SOME REFLECTIONS

"Desire doth outrun performance." By 1963 the Church of South India, in its fifteen dioceses, could boast of one hundred and twenty-nine full-time paid deacons (of whom forty-nine were in one diocese) and twenty-five honorary deacons (of whom ten were in one diocese). Most of the paid deacons were men serving a short probation for the presbyterate. It is clear that neither the idea of the diaconate as a life-long vocation nor the idea of honorary deacons has yet, to any great extent, caught the imagination of suitable individuals or won the enthusiasm of diocesan committees.

It is clear, too, that only small progress has been made towards increasing the degree of ministerial pastoral care for village congregations now so largely dependent upon unordained church workers and lay volunteers. In the fifteen dioceses there are over 8,000 congregations but only about 850 paid presbyters in pastoral work and 46 honorary presbyters. Even these figures do not show the real extent to which the villages still lack adequate ministerial care, as the ordained ministry is naturally concentrated, to a considerable extent, in the large town and city congregations, where there are more educated people, and which can provide the whole or the greater part of a minister's salary. Even of the honorary presbyters, more than two-thirds, and of the honorary deacons, three-quarters, are said to be serving in towns.

It is not surprising that there should be a wide gap and time-lag between the thinking of leaders of the Church and local committees in a country like South India where in many parts there is still much illiteracy, and where many local leaders, and even members of diocsan councils, have little knowledge of either the practices or the problems of the Church beyond their own localities.

But it may be thought also that the leaders of the Church in its central committees are perhaps too much inclined to theoretical considerations and pay too little attention to practical needs. After all, *diakonia* loses its meaning if it is not closely related to the practical needs of the people who are to be served; and these needs vary greatly, both in different areas and amongst different classes of Christians, and even among the same people at different periods of their development in the Christian life, in educational and economic level, and in their social environment. In all these matters, as well as in such matters as the relative size of congregations and the distances between them, there are the widest differences in the various rural areas of the vast territory covered by the Church of South India, while conditions in the large cities and fast developing new industrial areas again are totally different from those in rural areas. It would seem unlikely, *prima facie*, that any particular detailed scheme could usefully be imposed upon the Church as a whole. There should be local experiment and much freedom given to dioceses and within dioceses, in developing the particular forms of *diakonia* locally appropriate. The realization of this lies behind the recurrent action of the synod in referring recommendations of its committees to the dioceses for study, comment, and experiment, instead of proceeding to their adoption as rules of the whole Church.

The greatest need is for adequate provision of the full ministry of both word and sacrament, and this will be possible financially in many rural areas, at least in the foreseeable future, only by the development of a local honorary presbyterate. An increase in the diaconate, either paid or honorary, does not meet the need for the sacraments.

In cities and towns, where presbyters are relatively more numerous than in rural areas and where congregations are larger, there is a much stronger case both for a permanent diaconate and for a larger number of honorary deacons to assist the presbyters and to relieve them of some of the duties that now fall upon them. But unless the functions of the diaconate can be more clearly distinguished from those of presbyters on the one hand, and of lay deacons, lay readers, lay preachers, and paid catechists on the other hand, the office of deacon is unlikely to have a wide appeal as a worthwhile, life-long vocation. Some men ordained with a view to life-time service as deacons before long press for ordination to the presbyterate, and village congregations served by a deacon are only too ready to support the plea. It may be pointed out also that the liturgical functions associated with the diaconate, and which may enrich the idea of the diaconate as fulfilling the ministry of Christ in his Church to temporal and bodily needs, can hardly possess this significance in the minds of the people unless there are deacons in numbers adequate to ensure their presence at most services of Holy Communion. If the "deacon's part" in the Holy Communion service is usually taken by either a presbyter or a layman, the liturgical argument for the ordained diaconate ceases to have much meaning.

Considering all these factors, and considering the immense value and influence of honorary lay service, and that the witness and influence of such service tend to be diminished when laymen by ordination become "professionals," even if in an honorary capacity, it may in the end be questioned whether it is not the ordained diaconate, rather than the Congregational type of lay diaconate or the Presbyterian eldership, that needs to be justified.

V. ADDITIONAL NOTE ON ORDINATION OF MISSIONARIES

A particular problem which has exercised the Church of South India from time to time may be of interest, since it arises from the circumstance of the C.S.I. being a united Church receiving missionaries from both Anglican and non-Anglican Churches overseas, and may recur in such union Churches elsewhere.

It was agreed before union that during the first thirty years ministers of the parent Churches of the originally separate parts would be received as ministers on accepting the governing principles and constitution and being commissioned by prayer without the laying on of hands. After this period the Church is to decide for itself on what terms it will receive into its ministry ministers of other Churches. But since the union a practice has developed, especially by some of the non-episcopal societies, of sending out young missionaries unordained, though fully qualified for ordination in their home Churches. This practice has been encouraged by the Church of South India as being in line with its desire fully to unify its ministry. Men coming out already ordained are subject to the pledge given before union, not to impose on any congregation an unaccustomed form of ministry to which it conscientiously objects. This pledge, vital at the time of union, has hardly ever had to be invoked, partly owing to care in stationing men in suitable pastorates, and partly owing to the growing together of the different parts of the Church. But no conscientious objection can be raised to ministers ordained within the united Church. It is not surprising that the deferment of their ordination so that it may take place in South India has been desired also by many young missionaries themselves. It means that their orders are acceptable both throughout the Church of South India and also in all the parent Churches.

The problem has arisen whether these men should first be ordained to the diaconate. The considerations to be reconciled are the desire to encourage the practice of such men being ordained in South India, the desire that as far as possible the same rules for ordination should apply to missionaries as to Indians and also to missionaries from different denominations, and the desire to recognize special circumstances, deal fairly with the men concerned, and satisfy the rules and desires of their home Churches. The Synod, in 1960, resolved that missionaries should not be ordained by the Church of South India without agreement with the home Church or missionary society concerned, and assurance that the ordination would not raise difficulties when the missionary returned permanently to his own country.

The difficulty has been felt chiefly in connection with Methodist missionaries. British Methodism, though it has no probationary, ordained diaconate, normally ordains men only six years after they have been accepted as candidates. Three or four years of theological training are followed by two or three years as probationers or "ministers on trial." They are then given full ministerial status by being "received into full connexion" at the annual conference, and are ordained at a service on the evening of the same day. Formerly, missionaries were allowed to complete their probation abroad, but in 1961 the British Conference decided that, in view of the life-long responsibility undertaken for the employment and support of all ministers received into full connection, and in view of the return of not a few missionaries to work in Britain after a few years' service abroad, all men should complete their probation and be received into full connection before going abroad to serve in another Church. The Conference, while willing to postpone the ordination service of men going to serve in the Church of South India, desires that ordination to the full ministry should follow as closely as possible upon their being received into full connection; that is, soon after arrival in India.

In March, 1962, the Working Committee of the C.S.I. Synod advised bishops to ordain newly-appointed Methodist missionaries as deacons on arrival, and as presbyters when they had passed their first language examination. It added: "It is understood, of course, that each bishop and diocese will have to be satisfied that the missionary is fitted and suited to be ordained as a presbyter of the Church of South India as well as a Methodist minister of the British Conference." The Synod Executive Committee, meeting six months later, passed a resolution desiring that Methodist missionaries should spend at least twelve months before being ordained as presbyters, during which they could learn an Indian language and study conditions in India and the Indian Church. It added, "To satisfy this desire, the Methodist Missionary Society may consider the possibility of counting the first year spent in India as the last year of probation and send their missionaries to South India about twelve months before they are due to be received into full connexion by the British Methodist Conference." But this suggestion was considered incompatible with the policy of the Conference.

It was pointed out that the postponement of ordination to the presbyterate for a year or more after arrival, while superficially putting missionaries in the same position as Indians, actually imposes an additional probationary period on men who have already completed a probation more lengthy than the period usually spent by Indians in the diaconate. It would also put Methodist missionaries at a disadvantage in seniority as compared both with their Methodist contemporaries serving in

Britain and also with missionaries from some other traditions coming to serve in South India. The resolutions were criticized also as confusing fitness for ministerial status with probation to test suitability for missionary work in South India, which could be continued after ordination. After correspondence and personal consultation with the Asia Secretary of the Methodist Missionary Society, a mutually agreeable solution was reached when the synod in January 1964, resolved:

> where Methodist ministers appointed for missionary service in South India have satisfactorily completed their ministerial probation, extending over a period of six years, in their home Church, and have been received into Full Connexion by the Methodist Conference thus authorizing their immediate ordination to the full ministry of the Church, this period of probation shall be considered as equivalent to the Church of South India Diaconate, and on the authority of an official letter from the President of the Conference indicating that the Conference which would have ordained these men has deferred their ordination in deference to the Church of South India, so that they may be ordained in accordance with the Order of the Church of South India, they shall be ordained as presbyters as soon as possible after their arrival in S. India, allowing suitable time for preparation.

The resolution, of course, failed to grapple with the underlying theological issue that concerns the significance of the act of ordination in these circumstances. The correspondence made it clear that the Methodist Conference regards these men as ordained to the Methodist ministry by the Church of South India, acting as the agent of the Methodist Conference, and on its responsibility. The Church of South India supposes itself to be ordaining them as ministers of the Church of South India. It does not regard them merely as ministers of another Church lent for service, but as an integral part of its own ministry. Nor do many in the Church of South India feel quite happy at ordaining men whose fitness it has had no adequate time to judge, merely, as it were, rubber-stamping the decision of another Church. Can a man simultaneously be a minister of two autonomous churches? Does it really matter very much? After all, the British Methodist Church and the Church of South India are in relations of full communion. And in the Ordinal of the latter it is said that, "We speak and act as part of the One, Holy, Catholic, and Apostolic Church," and after the prayer and act of ordination the ordinand is declared to be now a presbyter "in the Church of God." The only specific reference to the Church of South India is in the question, "Seeing you believe you are called to exercise this ministry within the Church of South India, will you accept its discipline . . . ?"

It may be added that this Synod passed also a resolution permitting missionaries of the Church of Scotland, who have been licensed by a presbytery at home, to be ordained directly to the presbyterate soon after their arrival in India.

MARY P. TRUESDELL

THE OFFICE OF DEACONESS

I. THE HISTORY OF THE OFFICE: THE BEGINNING

All Christian vocation and ministry has its beginning with our Lord Jesus Christ. The starting point of the office of deaconess is with him, and his relation to the women of his day. He afforded woman a higher place than she had ever had before.

In the Orient, woman was a mere possession of man, a chattel. In Greece, her life was one of seclusion and obscurity. In Rome, more honor was paid women, but they were under the absolute domination of their fathers and later their husbands. Although the position of woman was higher among the Hebrews, and there were several rare women who had the gift of prophecy, yet a Jewish man still blesses God who has not made him "a gentile, a slave, . . . or a woman." Women could only enter into the outer parts of the Temple; they were excused from keeping a great deal of the Law; their vows could be voided by husband or father, and their word was not taken at law. They were respected and honored in home life, but looked upon as inferior. When in the fullness of time God sent his Son, Christ humbled himself to be born of a woman, whom all generations shall call blessed.

Throughout his ministry, our Lord showed an especial tenderness toward women and children. He condemned the prevailing idea of divorce, and proposed a high and sacred concept of marriage. His compassion for the widow is reflected in parable and miracle. Though weary, he stopped when mothers brought their children to him for blessing. Women came to him for healing and in penitence. Women sat at his feet to hear his words. His disciples often wondered at the respect he had for women, both bad and good. He was different from other rabbis. When he went about preaching and proclaiming the glad tidings of the kingdom, not a few women ministered to him of their substance. At the foot of the Cross, faithful women stood until the end, when all but one of his chosen twelve had forsaken him and fled; and they followed those who carried Jesus' body to its burial, and went home to prepare spices and ointments for its anointing.

That this loving service was agreeable to the mind of Christ, we may learn from his choosing the same faithful women to become the first witnesses of his glorious resurrection.

That the Son of God had a definite plan for the continuing of his presence and ministry after the necessary withdrawal of his visible, physical presence from the earth, is shown by his institution of the sacraments, and the choosing and training of the twelve. Before the end of his earthly ministry, the Lord ordained and commissioned them. "As my Father hast sent me, even so send I you" (Jn 20,21). "Go into all the world . . ." (Mk 16,15). The developing details of this ministry of reconciliation were to be worked out under the guidance of the holy Spirit. "These things," said our Lord, "have I spoken unto you, being yet present with you. But the Comforter, the Holy Ghost whom the Father will send in my name, he shall teach you all things and bring all things to your remembrance" (Jn 14, 25-26).

II. THE APOSTOLIC TIMES

"When the day of Pentecost was fully come, they were all with one accord in one place. And suddenly . . . they were all filled with the Holy Ghost . . . " (Acts 2,1 ff). The faithful women were in the company, and these women no less than men were partakers of the special gifts of the Spirit. St. Luke cites this as the fulfillment of the ancient prophecy of Joel, (Joel 2,28-29), quoted by St. Peter: "I will pour out my Spirit upon all flesh and your sons and daughters shall prophesy . . . upon the servants and handmaidens in those days will I pour out my Spirit" (Acts 2,17 f.).

The Church's ministry grew out of the Church's need. With the multiplying of the number of disciples, the twelve soon realized they alone could not manage all the details, particularly those attendant upon the daily ministrations of charity. So that the apostles should give themselves continually to prayer and to the ministry of the word of God, they gave direction for the choosing of seven men, "full of the Holy Ghost and wisdom." The seven were set apart to attend to these practical matters, to "serve (*diakonein*) tables" (Acts 6,1-6). The seven are nowhere called by the title deacon, but they were appointed to their duties with prayer and the laying on of hands by the apostles. This marked the beginning of a differentiated ministry, and has always been taken by the Church as the embryonic beginning of the office of deacon.

The use of the word deacon (and later deaconess) as a title came as a gradual crystallization of an everyday Greek word of common gender, which literally meant "servant." But this Greek word had a slightly different meaning from our English term. There were other words in Greek that denoted service for pay, and the duty service of a slave. But the noun and corresponding verb *diakonein* meant service freely and lovingly given and are used throughout the New Testament, in speaking of the service of St. Martha, of St. Peter's mother-in-law, of the angels, and of the ministry of the women to Jesus. Our Lord used it also when he said, "I came not to be ministered unto (*diakonethenai*), but to minister (*diakonesai*)" (Mt 20,28). "I am among you as he that serveth (*diakonon*)" (Lk 22,27). Literally, "I am among you as a deacon."

The first place where we find the word used as a title is apparently in Romans 16,1-2. St. Paul, writing to the Roman Christians in about the year 56 or 58 A.D., says:

I commend unto you Phoebe, our sister, which is a deacon (*diakonon*) of the Church[1] which is in Cenchrea: that ye receive her in the Lord, as becometh saints, and that ye assist her in whatsoever business she hath need of you: for she hath been a succourer of many, and of myself also.

At this early time, we cannot read into the use of the word the full meaning connoted in a later day. But we can certainly gather from St. Paul's words that Phoebe seems to have been doing a ministering service. Cenchrea was a mere village some nine miles from Corinth and its southern port, from which St. Paul embarked on his second missionary journey. The rough harbor town was probably quite a contrast to the intellectual, wealthy, and luxury-loving Corinth. St. Paul had spent eighteen months in the city, and it is possible that Phoebe was one of his converts there, and when a mission had been planted in Cenchrea that she went there to serve. St. Paul speaks of her as "a" deacon, rather than "the" deacon, so there may have been others. Tradition makes her the bearer of this important letter to Rome. Evidently she was a woman of means and generosity. St. Paul's words speak well of her character and bravery in setting out on an arduous and long journey; his request that the Romans assist her in whatsoever she had need, shows she must have had executive ability, perhaps going to Rome on a business mission.

The next use of the title deacon is in the pastoral epistles. Whether written by St. Paul to St. Timothy about the year 61 A.D. after his release from his first imprisonment, or whether written later by another person, "The Pastor," we find Church orders emerging into a little more definite form. In I Timothy 3, 8-12, in the middle of a passage about deacons, the writer lists qualifications likewise for women. The import of the passage has long been obscured by the erroneous translation of the word "women" (*gunaikas*) as "their wives." There is no pronoun in the Greek text. *Diakonos* being a common gender noun, to make himself clear the writer inserted the word "women" when speaking especially about the women deacons. The writer's meaning can be easily seen when the text is arranged in parallel columns thus:

| Likewise must the deacons be grave, not double-tongued, not given to much wine not greedy of filthy lucre, holding the mystery of the faith in a pure conscience. | Likewise must women be grave, not slanderers, sober, ... full of faith in all things. |

The men deacons dispensed the alms, a function which evidently the women deacons did not have at this early time, hence the caution to men deacons against greed.

Was the office of deaconess of apostolic origin? Assuredly, yes. Bishop Lightfoot wrote: "As I read my New Testament, the female diaconate is quite as definite an institution as the male diaconate."[2] Dean Howson asserts: "It appears to me that if we take our stand simply on the ground of the New Testament, the argument for the recognition of the deaconess as a part of the Christian ministry is as strong as the argument for the episcopacy."[3] There have been some who disliked the idea that women ever had any part in the ministry of the Church and who tried to prove that the office of deaconess was of late development, while the office of deacon existed from the beginning in quite definite form. Critical study of the New-Testament age seems to show that *all* Church orders were rudimentary at the time. At the time of St. Timothy, a bishop was more of an overseer than the monarchial bishop of later centuries. The office of presbyter was rather vague as to duties, and the deacons were the "men-servants" and "women-servants" who took care of the charitable work of the Church. The important thing is that in the apostolic age, when the great outpouring of the Holy Spirit at Pentecost was still a dynamic experience, the Church made its beginning of a differentiated ministry and guided the initial developments.

III. THE PRE-NICENE PERIOD

The first reference to deaconesses outside the New Testament occurs in a letter written about the year 112 A.D. by Pliny, Roman Governor of Bithynia, to the Emperor Trajan, asking how to deal with the Christian sect.[4] In trying to discover what the Christians were doing, he had put to the torture two hand-maidens who were called ministers (deaconesses), *"ancillae quae vocantur ministrae."* Ministrae was the Latin translation of the Greek *diakonoi.*

Clement of Alexandria (155-220 A.D.) was head of the Alexandrian catechetical school, which was a center of Christian theology in the second and third centuries. He was a learned student of Scripture, and it is interesting to note that he interprets St. Paul's rules (I Tim 3,11) as referring to the ministry of women (*diakonon gunaikon*).[5] Origen (185-254 A.D.), teacher and philosopher, a pupil and successor of Clement as head of the Alexandrian school for a while, whose study of the Scriptures entitles him to rank as the father of biblical criticism, comments on Romans 16,1-2, and asserts this shows that women were also established in the ministry (*diakonia*) of the Church.[6]

While these two writers do not speak as if they knew of deaconesses existing in their time and locality, they were not unacquainted with the use of these Greek words as meaning a title to a specific ministry of women in the Church.

The *Apostolic Didascalia,* a document dated in the second half of the third or beginning of the fourth century, was probably written originally in Greek and has been preserved in a Syriac translation. It gives us a picture of Church order of these early times, and contains a startling metaphor that reveals that the writer had a very high conception of the diaconate of women. It also shows why deaconesses were needed, and how they were used. In Chapter 17, we read:

> Wherefore, O Bishop, thou shalt appoint unto thee laborers of righteousness, helpers with thee unto life. Those that seem good to thee out of all the people thou shalt choose and appoint Deacons, a man for the doing of many things that are needed, and a woman for the ministration to the women. For there are houses where thou canst not send the Deacon unto women because of the heathen; but thou shalt send the Deaconess. For also in many other things the Office of a woman [that is, a Deaconess] is required.[7]

The *Apostolic Constitutions* tell of Church practices perhaps a century or so later than the Syriac *Didascalia*, both before and after Nicaea. The deaconess is mentioned after the deacon and before the subdeacon. The imposition of hands by the bishop is spoken of as the accepted method of making deaconesses. A prayer from the *Constitution* is embodied into some of the modern admission rites:

> Concerning Deaconesses . . .
> O Bishop, thou shalt lay thy hands upon her, with the Presbytery and the Deacons and Deaconesses standing by; and thou shalt say:
> "Eternal God, the Father of our Lord Jesus Christ, the Creator of man and woman, that didst fill with the Spirit Mary (Miriam) and Deborah, and Anna and Hulda, that didst not disdain that thine only begotten Son should be born of a woman; thou that in the tabernacle of witness and in the temple didst appoint the women guardians of thy holy gates: Do thou look on this thy handmaid, which is appointed unto ministry [or "unto the Office of Deaconess"] (*eis diakonian*); and grant unto her the holy Spirit, and cleanse her from all pollution of the flesh and of the spirit, that she may worthily accomplish the work committed unto her, to thy glory and the praise of thy Christ, with whom to thee and the holy Spirit be glory and worship world without end. Amen.[8]

From these early documents and others, including the *Testament of Our Lord* (fourth or fifth century), we learn of the functions performed by the deaconesses of the early Church:

1. The assisting at the administration of the baptism of women. "It is required that those who go down into the water (of baptism) shall be anointed with the oil of anointing by a deaconess."

2. Instructing newly baptized women. "When she that is baptized cometh up from the water, the deaconess shall receive her, and shall teach her and instruct her how the seal of baptism may be unbroken in chastity and holiness."

3. The taking of messages of the bishop to women, where he could not send the deacon.

4. Ministering to the sick and poor.

5. Ministering to the martyrs in prison.

6. Presiding over the women's entrance into the church; examining the commendatory letters of strangers and assigning them places.

7. Oversight of the widows and orphans.

8. The taking of the Eucharist to women who were sick.[9]

IV. THE GENERAL CHURCH COUNCILS

Nicea, 325 A.D. The clergy of the heretical Paulianist sect returning to the Catholic fold were required by the council to be rebaptized and reordained. The same rule was to be observed concerning deaconesses, who were specially mentioned since some of them wearing the habit had not received the laying on of hands and therefore were to be considered laity (canon XIX).[10]

Chalcedon, 451 A.D. (The fourth general council.) The ordination of deaconesses is expressly called both *cheirotoneisthai* and *cheirothesia*—ordination by the imposition of hands (canon XV).[11]

Trullo, 692 A.D. (Called "Quinisext" as being supplemental to the fourth and fifth councils, which were occupied wholly with matters of faith.) This council speaks of the ordination of deaconesses in two canons (XIV and XLVIII) using the word *cheirotoneisthai*. While Pope Sergius did not approve six of the canons of this council, the canons on deaconesses were accepted.[12]

V. THE OFFICE OF DEACONESS IN THE EASTERN CHURCH

The order developed in numbers and prestige in the Eastern Church, reaching its height in the fourth, fifth, and sixth centuries. "All the leading Greek Fathers and Church writers of the age—St. Basil (326-379 A.D.), St. Gregory of Nyssa (died 396 A.D.), Epiphanius (died 403 A.D.), Chrysostom (344-407 A.D.), Theodoret (393-457 A.D.), Sozomen (5th century) refer to it, and notices of individual deaconesses become frequent in Church annals, whilst everywhere the female diaconate is spoken of as an honorable office, and one filled by persons of rank, talent, and fortune."[13]

St. John Chrysostom, bishop of Constantinople, spoke out so eloquently against the sins of the emperor and the moral laxity of clergy and laity alike that he was forced to flee into exile. There were forty deaconesses on the staff of the cathedral of St. Sophia, and they helped the bishop to escape. The burning of the cathedral the next day was laid to their charge and they were cruelly treated. The exiled bishop wrote letters to them, comforting them, and congratulating them on their courage and patience. His many personal letters to these deaconesses give interesting glimpses of their lives and position.[14]

The codes and laws of the Emperor Justinian in the middle of the sixth century give considerable information as to the status of the deaconess.[15] The beautiful building of St. Sophia (now a mosque) was built by Justinian, and the number of clergy to be attached was fixed by law: one hundred deacons, and forty deaconesses at the cathedral; a small parish was allotted six deaconesses.

Deaconesses were considered members of the clergy in both civil and ecclesiastical law. They were ordained with the imposition of hands by the bishops, the same words being used to describe the rite whether administered to the man or woman deacon. In the parallel services for the ordination of deacon and deaconess found in the *Apostolic Constitutions*, though the two ordination prayers vary, the same word is used regarding the office to which both are admitted, and prayer is made that the Holy Spirit be granted to each:

Deacon.	Deaconess.
Almighty God . . . make thy face to shine upon this thy servant which is appointed unto the office of deacon [*eis diakonian*], and fill him with the Spirit, and with power . . .	Eternal God . . . look on this thy handmaid, which is appointed unto the office of deaconess [*eis diakonian*], and grant unto her the holy Spirit . . .[16]

In the Constantinopolitan Rite of the service books of the Eastern Church, the prayer that accompanies the laying on of hands in the ordination of a deaconess runs thus:

> O Lord God, who does not reject women who offer themselves in accordance with the divine will to minister in thy holy places, but admittest them into the rank of ministers [*leitourgoi*], give the grace of thy holy Spirit even to this thy handmaid, who desireth to offer herself to thee, and to fulfill the grace of the ministry as thou didst give the grace of thy ministry unto Phoebe. . . .

In this service in the Greek euchology, the bishop "puts the diaconal stole (*orarium*) on her neck, under the wimple (*maphorium*), bringing the two ends forward. . . . After she has partaken of the holy Body and Blood, the archbishop gives her the holy chalice, which she receives and puts back on the holy table."[17]

An early service in the Latin Church gives directions to the bishop for putting on the stole as he blesses the deaconess in the mass for the consecration of a deaconess.[18] In the pontifical of Egbert, archbishop of York (733-766 A.D.), there is an "Episcopal Benediction at the Ordination of a Deaconess."[19]

It is a justifiable conclusion that the diaconate these services were intended to confer was as real a diaconate as that conferred upon men. "That the deaconess never did all the work of a deacon does not show that her diaconate was not as real. There were obvious restrictions on account of her sex. In the period under consideration, nothing else would have been conceivable. But it was restriction of function due to sex and circumstance, not a defect or absence of order. A parallel restriction is equally obvious in the case of a deacon, who would not *normally* anoint a woman at Baptism—that is, if a deaconess could be had."[20]

The deaconess received the Eucharist directly after the clergy, and was addressed by such terms as "most reverend" and "the venerable." The deaconess was considered of higher rank than the subdeacon. The minor orders were not of apostolic origin but developed later. They did not employ the laying on of hands at first, and hence were called *acheirotonetos uperesia* or *insacrati ministri*.[21] In later years, as the office of deacon grew in importance, and together with it the office of subdeacon, the laying on of hands was administered to the subdeacon. As the office of deaconess diminished in numbers and functions, it became ranked below that of subdeacon.

VI. THE OFFICE OF DEACONESS IN THE WESTERN CHURCH

In the West, deaconesses were not as numerous, nor do we find early evidence that this office was much used. The great Latin

Fathers Ambrose, Jerome, and Augustine are silent on the subject, but we know that the existence of the office was not unknown in Rome because Rome was represented in the great ecumenical councils. The Council of Nicaea recognized the order as a matter of course.[22]

Conditions of oriental society created a need for deaconesses and their ministry that did not obtain in the West. Accordingly, we find younger widows—not pensioners of the Church—doing some active work in the Western Church; but these were not deaconesses and the distinction is quite clear.

The first mention of deaconesses in the West occurs in 394 A.D., when a local synod (Nimes) forbade further ordination of them;[23] possibly the order had recently been introduced into Gaul from the East. There followed other prohibition by other local synods (Orange, 441, Epâon, 517), and severe penalties against the marriage of a deaconess by the synod of Orleans in 533. We may judge that local prohibitions had little effect on an institution sanctioned by the general Church, for we have the record of some deaconesses in the West. For example, in 530 the influential and saintly bishop of Rheims, St. Remigius, left a bequest to "my blessed daughter Hilaria, the deaconess,"[24] and in 539 in Pavia, "Theodora, the deaconess, of blessed memory" was buried.[25]

In 544 we have the interesting story of the ordination of the deaconess St. Rhadegund. She was a Thuringian princess who was captured as a child by Clothaire I, a Frankish king, and later forced into marriage with him, becoming one of his seven recognized wives. He was a violent and wicked man. Rhadegund, who had learned the Christian faith, fled from court after the King's treacherous murder of her brother and sought refuge at Noyon where she entreated the bishop, St. Medard, to ordain her a deaconess. The demand was entirely irregular, and the bishop at first refused on the ground that her married state disqualified her for the diaconate. With the pursuing king and his warriors at the door of the church, she hurried to the sacristy, and laying aside her rich clothing and jeweled girdle, donned a religious habit she found hanging there, returned to the altar and said to the bishop: "If thou shalt refuse to consecrate me, and shall fear men rather than God, let the soul of the sheep be required of the shepherd at thy hand!" Smitten by this solemn adjuration, he laid his hands upon her and consecrated her a deaconess (*manu superposita consecravit eam diaconam*).

Through the mediation of another bishop, Germanus, the king was induced to consent to a separation, and the deaconess Rhadegund retired to Poitiers, where she founded a convent. She herself was not the abbess, but lived as a simple nun, renowned for her saintliness, and consulted by rulers of state. One of her friends was the poet, Bishop Fortunatus, who is known to us by some very familiar hymns he wrote: "The royal banners forward go," "Hail, Festal Day," "Welcome, happy morning," and others. Their's was a beautiful friendship, and many little gifts of fruit and flowers were sent from the convent to the bishop. When deaconess Rhadegund died in 587, she was buried with great honor by Gregory, bishop of Tours. Bishop Fortunatus wrote an account of her life.[26]

Deaconesses were in Rome in the eighth century, if not before. We find a votive tablet erected to the deaconess Anna by her twin brother Dometius, deacon and treasurer of the Holy See. When Pope Leo III and Charlemagne entered Rome in triumph in 799, they were met by "the Roman populace, including nuns, deaconesses, and noble matrons."[27] In the eleventh century we find charters of four popes issued to bishops in Italy, which state the right of the bishops "to make priests, deacons, deaconesses, and subdeacons."[28]

VII. THE DECLINE OF THE OFFICE

After the sixth century the order began to decline, both in numbers and in prestige. It was never abolished, however; it simply ceased to function. The reasons for this were several.

The conditions of society had changed. As the Church moved westward, men were less restricted in their ministration to women. The new freedom accorded women in the early days of Christianity was lost. The decline and breakup of the Roman Empire made it unsafe for women to live and work alone, and hence the protection of the cloister became necessary for them to live a consecrated life.

The rise of the monastic orders confused and absorbed many of the distinctive characteristics of the order of deaconess. Deaconess communities adopted monastic ideas, and instead of being the direct servant of the bishop, the deaconess pledged obedience first of all to the superior of the order. Bishops often named a deaconess as abbess in charge of a community of lay women or "choir of virgins," because the deaconess by virtue of her office was under episcopal control, and religious orders were often a little too independent of that control. All abbesses were not deaconesses, but there is confusion of terms.

There was a gradual change from the conception of the early diaconate. The office of deacon began to grow in importance, and to lose its early characteristic as an office dedicated to life-long service. Instead it became a stepping-stone to a higher office, a sort of sub-priesthood, as it really is in the Church today. Many duties performed by deacon and deaconess in the early days were delegated to the subdeacon and the lesser orders. The Church failed to adapt the office of deaconess to new tasks as former duties were laid aside. Baptism of adults became rare; immersion was abandoned as a method of baptism; martyrs were no longer imprisoned; and men and women no longer sat in separate places in the Church.

During the Middle Ages, the mind of the Church largely centered on individual salvation, ascetic practices, and theological problems. Ministering to the poor and desolate took a relatively minor place; the charitable work that was done was performed almost exclusively by the monastic communities.

VIII. INTERESTING SURVIVALS

Several liturgical vestiges of the office of deaconess neverthe-less survived. In the pontifical of Egbert, archbishop of York (732-766), there is an episcopal benediction of a deacon or a deaconess, and also the benediction at the ordination of a deaconess.[29] In the Leofric missal of the bishop of Exeter (1050-1072), is a service for the making of a deaconess. This is contained in an appendix to the pontifical of Bainbridge, 1508.[30] In the Syrian Church, the prayer for the consecration of a bishop contains this petition, "that through the power of the gift [of the Holy Ghost] he may make priests, deacons, subdeacons and deaconesses for the ministry of thy holy Church."[31]

In the Roman Catholic Church there is a direct survival, though it represents the medieval rather than primitive type of deaconess. In the Carthusian order, which came into exist-ence in the twelfth century, and which has three houses of nuns in France, Italy, and Belgium and numbers about 140 nuns, the diocesan bishop has continued to "consecrate into the place of deaconess" some of the older professed nuns. They are vested with stole and maniple which is worn on the right arm, and the bishop uses "the same words that he says at the ordination of a deacon or subdeacon."[32] A nun thus consecrated sings the epistle at conventual high mass, though without leaving her place in the choir. If no priest be present at matins, a con-secrated nun assumes the stole and reads the Gospel.

Among the Benedictines and Cistercians the practice of "consecrating" nuns continued until the eighteenth century. Among some of the other orders three different veils were be-stowed: the veil of *profession* given as early as at twelve years of age, the veil of *consecration* given as early as twenty-five, and the veil of *ordination* given at forty. This last veil seems to be a survival of the ordination of a deaconess, since forty years was the usual requirement of the canons of the early Church for ordination to that office.[33]

IX. THE REVIVAL OF THE DEACONESS IN THE
MODERN CHURCH

Several factors led up to and influenced the restoration to usefulness of this ancient Church office. In 1625, St. Vincent de
Paul aroused interest in the poor and sick, and founded a new
type of religious order. His Sisters of Charity had at the beginning an uncloistered freedom and an ideal of service similar
to that of the primitive diaconate. He told his sisters: "Your
convent must be the houses of the sick, your cell the chamber
of suffering, your chapel the parish church, your cloister
the streets of the city."[34] Although this order later conformed
more to the usual monastic pattern, it did have its influence in
bringing to the forefront the ideal of service.

In 1734, the non-juring bishops of Scotland were led by
their study of Christian antiquities to desire the revival of the
office of deaconess. A service for the making of deaconesses
was compiled which was very complete and beautiful, in full
accord with ancient tradition, and providing for the laying on
of hands.[35] There is no evidence, however, that this service
was ever used.

A hundred years passed. The early nineteenth century saw
an awakened interest in the condition of the poor, first on the
part of many gifted women and then on the part of the Church
itself. The distressing social conditions created by industrial revolution underscored the profound need for women's pastoral
care.

In 1833, a Lutheran pastor, the Reverend Theodore
Fliedner, undertook to revive the ministry of deaconess for the
care of the unfortunate. An association of women was formed
at Kaiserwerth, Germany, that resembled St. Vincent de Paul's
sisterhood. The members received "consecration" at the hands
of pastors, according to the Lutheran idea of orders. This was
not considered ordination. This noble work grew to large pro-
portions, and has had a tremendous influence upon women's
work, and upon the care of the sick and old, the young and

destitute. Florence Nightingale received inspiration and training at Kaiserwerth, and the uniform and cap of the present-day nurse survive as reminders of the debt owed to the Lutheran deaconesses.

The successful work at Kaiserwerth also stimulated thought in England and America. There were several attempts in these countries to organize parochial and diocesan deaconess-sisterhoods, small communities after the Lutheran pattern.[36] Conceptions of the terms "deaconess" and "sister" were hazy; these devoted women were neither "religious" sisters nor were they true deaconesses in the technical meaning of the term. They were admitted to their communities by giving the right hand as pledge, whereas the *sine qua non* of the historic office of deaconess is the imposition of episcopal hands. But out of some of these experiments emerged true monastic communities, and the real restoration of the office of deaconess.

Under the wise leadership and careful study of antiquities by such men as Dean Howson, Bishop Lightfoot, Bishop Thorold, Canon Body, and others, when the office of deaconess was finally restored in the Church of England, it was done in accordance with primitive Catholic tradition, which differed quite essentially from the Lutheran pattern. In 1862, Bishop Tait of London admitted Elizabeth Ferard to the office of deaconess with the imposition of hands. She thus became the first woman to hold this historic office in England after the lapse of several centuries.

One of the first persons in America to have a true and clear concept of the office was Bishop Cobbs, the first Episcopal Bishop of Alabama. He planned a cathedral to be built at Montgomery with a group of institutions around it, including a house for deacons who were to do missionary work and assist in pastoral ministrations, and a house for deaconesses who were to teach and take care of the sick and poor. The plan reminds us of St. John Chrysostom's cathedral. "Such a plan," said Bishop Cobbs, "would enable a bishop to be, not simply the chairman of convention, but the heart, the motive power, and the controlling agent of his diocese—a bishop in the Gospel sense of the word."[37] The plan never materialized, probably because of the imminence of the Civil War.

Bishop Cobbs was succeeded by his friend, Bishop Richard Hooker Wilmer, who, late in December 1864, "instituted" as deaconesses—without the imposition of hands—three godly women who offered themselves for whatever work the bishop might assign them. The war had left many orphans, so the little community was put to work at once to take care of them. The group organized as a little sisterhood or community after the Kaiserwerth pattern, with a constitution and rules approved by the bishop. Although Bishop Wilmer did not at first use the laying on of hands in his service of "institution," he did so as early as 1885.[38] Two deaconesses were set apart that year: Deaconess Mary W. Johnson on Epiphany 1885 and Deaconess Mary Caroline Friggell on St. Peter's Day. Bishop Henry Codman Potter of New York set apart Julia Forneret as deaconess in 1887 with the imposition of hands.

Both Bishop Wilmer and Bishop Potter acted by their inherent rights as bishops of the historic Church.[39] In 1889, General Convention passed a canon authorizing the setting apart of deaconesses in the Episcopal Church.[40] After the passage of the canon, so anxious was Bishop Wilmer to have everything valid and canonical, that he called his little band of seven deaconesses together on the Feast of the Purification, 1893. Some of these had not received the laying on of hands; accordingly, in St. John's Church, Mobile, "in the face of a large congregation," he solemnly bestowed on each the imposition of hands.[41]

The Bishops of London, Alabama, and New York, in restoring the office before the specific canon had been passed, or authorization made, did nothing strange or amiss, for the ancient charters to bishops "concede and confirm the right to ordain bishops, priests, deacons, deaconesses, and subdeacons."

In restoring the office, the bishops have been extremely careful that the "Setting Apart Service" should have these *essential* parts: 1. Prayer; 2. The Laying on of Hands; 3. The Giving of Authority to a specific Office: "Take thou authority to execute the Office of Deaconess in the Church of God . . ." or "I admit thee to the Office of Deaconess in the . . ." Two other things are added now: the giving of the New Testament and the giving of the Deaconess Cross (added since the adoption of a uniform Cross in England and in America.)

X. THE TRAINING OF CANDIDATES IN THE EPISCOPAL CHURCH

After the Episcopal Church had officially recognized the revival of the ancient office with the passage of the deaconess canon in 1889, there was considerable interest and enthusiasm. Schools for training were started in various parts of the country —at San Francisco, New Orleans, Minneapolis, Philadelphia, New York, Berkeley, and Chicago. Several hundred women were trained and "set apart" into the office of deaconess, and quietly and humbly served in various capacities to the glory of God. Some were teachers, some nurses, some headed institutions for the care of children or the aged, some served in church settlement houses and in parochial work. In many lands, in many places, in the city, in the lonely country, with the rich, the poor, the delinquent, the troubled, deaconesses have labored and are laboring for Christ and his Church.

The Episcopal training schools that were started so ambitiously were of local or diocesan character and financial difficulties closed many of them within a relatively short time, but the schools in Philadelphia, New York, and Berkeley continued for many years. It was the plan of all these schools to train not only the deaconess candidates, but also other women who were preparing for missionary work or wished to serve as graduate trained workers. The candidates were in the majority at first, but as the years went on, the proportion changed, and the student body consisted mostly of those in general training. The schools in Berkeley and Philadelphia became general Church training schools, and lay women were placed in charge. The Philadelphia school united with Windham House, which had been created by the Woman's Auxiliary as a national graduate training center. These schools have had fine leadership and have done excellent work. But while it was true that a deaconess candidate could obtain most of the academic work that would prepare her to take her canonical examinations for the office of deaconess, this is but one side of the necessary preparation.

The candidate with a vocation to an office in the Church needs more than professional training. The work of a deaconess is arduous and often lonely; she needs a deep spiritual reservoir to draw from in the arid times. She is a spiritual shepherdess, particularly to the women and children of Christ's flock, the fortunate and the unfortunate needy souls. It is no easy task to go out in the name of the Church, expected to carry responsibility, yet to be willing to follow; to be strong physically, mentally, and spiritually, but never to fail in tenderness, sympathy, or helpfulness toward the weak, the simple, and the foolish. During the training period, her vocation must be nourished and developed and special training given in the ministration of the office. The Church would not attempt to prepare men to be deacons and priests in theological seminaries run entirely by laymen. Neither could the Church prepare deaconess candidates in schools run entirely by lay women, no matter how competent and able, nor how high the school's academic standing. The appreciation of the value of the ordination gift of grace is best transmitted by those who have received it.

The New York Training School for Deaconesses was the last of the diocesan schools where the training of candidates had been the primary purpose. Forced to close for financial reasons, it was reopened and run for several years by the deaconesses who raised enough money to augment endowment funds. Then came an unfortunate setback. By an old agreement with the diocese of New York, the building housing the school, built on the cathedral grounds, was needed for diocesan work, and had to be surrendered for this. Income from the endowment funds of the closed school is now used to assist the order with certain salaries and scholarship aid.

For a few years there was no place where a deaconess candidate could be trained with and by deaconesses. There were very few candidates and these were prepared privately under episcopal supervision or sent for preparation to a deaconess school in England.

The gravity of this situation was realized by many leaders in the Episcopal Church as well as by the deaconesses themselves. There was an urgent need that something be done. A school or college had to be established for the specialized training of candidates by and with deaconesses, or the order would soon cease to exist on this side of the Atlantic. This training center should be on a national foundation, not local or diocesan.

Early in 1953, Bishop Conkling of Chicago called a meeting of those who had comprised the last Advisory Commission on the Work of Deaconesses (1949-1952) to discuss the problem and formulate some plans. The result was the incorporation in Illinois of The Central House for Deaconesses. The bishops of Chicago, New York, and Alabama, the chancellor of Chicago, two priests, two deaconesses, and a lay woman were the incorporators, and served as the first board of trustees.

The first problem was to find a suitable location and building. Geographically central, Evanston, Illinois, was considered the best location, especially because of the educational facilities available. This was not immediately possible, and the trustees felt action was necessary, so they gladly accepted the offer of the bishop of Chicago to use a building at the Bishop McLaren Conference Center at Sycamore, Illinois. The building was rehabilitated and formally opened with the blessing of the house on October 29, 1953.

For the next five years, annual retreats and conferences were held, and candidates were trained or completed their preparation. But Sycamore was a difficult location geographically. When a small house was found in Evanston, it was purchased in 1958. This led to the acquiring of a larger house in 1960 in the desired location near university and seminary. The house belongs to the whole Episcopal Church. Six dioceses are represented on its board of trustees, and some of its maintenance comes from the budget of the national Church program. Though located within the diocese of Chicago, and gratefully appreciative for guidance and fostering care of this diocese, constant attention is called to the fact that the Central House for Deaconesses is a national, and not a diocesan project.

The Central House serves as headquarters for the deaconesses of the Church, and has proved of great value in this capacity, giving inspiration and promoting fellowship among the widely separated members of the order. Its training program has been flexible enough to adapt to changing times. With the opening of the seminaries to women students, candidates can best take the canonically required subjects at a seminary, and if qualified, work for an M.A. degree in Christian education, or for a B.D. degree. As an economy of time and strength, it has been found best for the candidates to live at the seminary, though in close touch with the Central House at all times. In Evanston, a mutually acceptable program has been worked out with Seabury-Western, and also with other seminaries. However, candidates are being prepared for something more than a profession, namely, a life-long vocation of ministry. The Central House still has an important part to play in developing that vocation and instructing in the history and ministration of the office. Therefore, an initial period of indoctrination is given candidates preliminary to seminary work, and for all candidates, wherever their preparation may have been, a period of final preparation before being ordained.

XI. STATUS OF THE OFFICE OF DEACONESS IN THE ANGLICAN COMMUNION

After the official restoration of the order of deaconesses, there was considerable confusion of thought. A century ago, there was great prejudice against women in any type of professional work, and this had its impact in ecclesiastical thinking. Historical data was not easy of access.

To meet this situation, the archbishop of Canterbury, in 1917, appointed a committee of clerical and lay scholars to delve into historical material regarding the ministry of women in the Church in earlier times, and that of deaconesses in particular. Their report[42] was thoroughly thrashed out in the Lambeth Conference of 1920. The resolutions adopted were quite definite. They were simplified and adopted by the 1930 Lambeth Conference and reaffirmed again in 1948, in the following terms:

> 114. The Conference reaffirms Resolution 67 of the Conference of 1930 that "the Order of Deaconess is for women the one and only Order of Ministry which we can recommend our branch of the Catholic Church to recognize and use." It also approves the resolution adopted 1939-1941 in both Houses of the Convocations of Canterbury and York "that the Order of Deaconesses is the one existing ordained ministry for women in the sense of being the only Order of Ministry in the Anglican Communion to which women are admitted by episcopal imposition of hands. . . .
>
> 116. The Conference desires to draw attention again to the wide and important range of work which may be entrusted to deaconesses by the constituted authorities of any province of the Anglican Communion; and recommends that in all parts of the Anglican Communion the work of deaconesses should be encouraged and their status and function defined.[43]

Subsequently, the Convocations of Canterbury and York made resolutions, later reaffirming them again, stating:

> Thus it becomes clear that while for men there is the threefold Holy Order of Bishops, Priests, and Deacons, for

women there is the Order of Deaconesses. This fact has its origins in history, for it is clear that within the Ministry of the Early Church, Deaconesses played an important part. This re-affirmation by the Convocations was needed to put to an end the misunderstandings which have existed for some time past regarding the nature and character of the Order. . . . At her ordination as a Deaconess, a woman receives by episcopal ordination a distinctive and permanent status in the Church and is dedicated to a life-long service and ministry.

In America, the 1919 General Convention appointed a "Commission on Adapting the Office of Deaconess to the Present Tasks of the Church." This Commission did a great deal of study of the Lambeth research and resolutions and as a result, the canon, "Of Deaconesses," was revised in 1922. It placed the order of deaconesses alongside of the other orders of ministry so regulated. As of General Convention of 1964, canon 50, "Of Deaconesses," reads: "Sec. 1. A woman of devout character and proved fitness, may be ordered Deaconess by any Bishop of this Church, subject to the provisions of this Canon.[44] The canon goes on to regulate the qualifications, candidacy, required subjects of study, age of admission, canonical examinations to be passed, testimonials of fitness of character, physical and mental health. No one can be recognized as a deaconess until the admission service is performed by the bishop. The deaconess must always be canonically attached to a diocese and under the direction of its bishop to whom an annual report must be made. Transfer to another diocese is by letters dimissory. The canon outlines the chief functions which may be entrusted to a deaconess. It also provides trial, for cause, in special ecclesiastical court as for other clergy.

To sum up: The resolutions of Lambeth, Canterbury and York, and the American canon make clear that the office of deaconess is a recognized part of the ordained ministry of the Church, but is now an order *sui generis*, not yet entirely returned to its ancient position.

XII. THE MINISTRY OF THE OFFICE OF DEACONESS

The ministerial duties of the office were outlined in very general terms in the early Episcopal Church's canon, yet beautifully summarized and expressed: "The duty of a Deaconess is: to teach the unlearned, to instruct youth, to care for the sick, to comfort the afflicted, to supply the wants of the poor and needy and to labor in all ways for the extension of the Church of Christ."[45] The present Canon is more specific:

Sec. 2 (a) The duty of a Deaconess is to assist in the work of the Parish, Mission, or institution to which she may be appointed, under the direction of the Rector or Priest in charge; or if there be none such, to perform such functions as may be directly entrusted to her by the Bishop.

(b) The following are the chief functions which may be entrusted to a Deaconess:

(1) The care of the sick, afflicted, and the poor;

(2) To give instruction in the Christian faith;

(3) Under the Rector or Priest in charge, to prepare candidates for Baptism and Confirmation.

(4) To assist at the administration of Holy Baptism and in the absence of the Priest or Deacon to baptize infants;

(5) Under the Rector or Priest in charge to organize, superintend and carry out the Church's work among women and children;

(6) With the approval of the Bishop and the incumbent, to read Morning and Evening Prayer (except such portions as are reserved for the Priest) and the Litany in Church or Chapel in the absence of the Minister; and when licensed by the Bishop to give instruction or deliver addresses at such services;

(7) To organize and carry on social work; and in colleges and schools to have a responsible part in the education of women and children and to promote the welfare of women students.[46]

XIII. WHAT OF THE FUTURE?

Is the office of deaconess outmoded? Should it be allowed to fade away quietly as a worthy "has been" of a past era? Or does the restored office present a *challenge* to the Church?

The office of deaconess is a great potential of help and vigor in the extension of the Church of Christ. In this age, when new fields are opening up to women, and their abilities are winning laurels in professional and scientific work, it is inconceivable that the Church would allow the secular world to absorb women's abilities. The office of deaconess is the modern answer to modern needs, yet set solidly within the framework of the historic apostolic ministry. Bishop Lightfoot wrote: "If the testimony borne in these two passages (Rom 16,1-2. and I Tim 3,11) to a ministry of women in Apostolic times had not been thus blotted out of our English Bibles, attention would probably have been directed to it at an earlier date, and our English Church would not have been remained so long maimed in one of her hands."[47]

The office of deaconess presents a challenge to be met by the best talents and abilities a woman may possess. It is not an easy life. It requires humility, sacrifice, and complete dedication. This is where the gift of grace in ordination helps. The gift is real and abiding. Though the going may be difficult at times, though the way be weary and tiring, there is the deep, inward, transcendent joy in the heart, which only those can know who hear the call of the Lord, and rise up to follow him into his harvest field!

THE DIACONATE: SACRED OR OUTMODED?

As every historian knows, prophecy is hazardous. Too often the historian has seen forecasts disproved by the event. In speculating on the future of the diaconate two approaches are possible; both are legitimate and do not necessarily conflict. One arises out of history. In view of the record across the centuries and contemporary trends, what developments seem fairly well assured? The other is basically theological. In light of the convictions out of which the diaconate arose, what guiding principles should govern that development?

Out of the history so competently sketched in the preceding chapters, some generalizations emerge. The first is that in one or another form, from the very beginning, the diaconate has been a feature of the Church. In a few of the many organizations in which those who profess and call themselves Christians have been enrolled, the diaconate as a distinct office has not existed. However, in the Churches which have embraced the overwhelming majority of those who bear the name Christian, the diaconate has invariably been present.

Out of the past comes another generalization. The functions and the relative importance of the diaconate have varied widely. That is true not only as between churches—as, for example, within the many bodies which constitute Protestantism, and those in what is usually called the Catholic tradition, including the Roman Catholic, the Orthodox, and the Anglican— but the variations have also been characteristic of most of the Churches, whether Protestant or Catholic, especially the latter, for each of them embodies a longer continuing tradition than the former, even when that tradition has been punctuated by crises and momentous transitions.

In all the Churches in which it exists the diaconate has become institutionalized, and the functions have repeatedly been altered. Sometimes, in both the Orthodox and Roman Churches and formerly in New England Congregationalism, they have been chiefly liturgical. Occasionally they have been mainly administrative, as for centuries in Rome, where the city was divided into seven ecclesiastical districts, each under a deacon, as against the fourteen civil districts of imperial Rome with civil officials. In early centuries the deacons were often closer to the bishops than were the presbyters. At other times, as in Anglicanism in recent centuries, the diaconate has chiefly been a preliminary step to the priesthood. That tradition has been preserved in American Methodism, where the future elder (presbyter) is first ordained deacon. Today, notably in the Roman Catholic Church as one of the fruits of Vatican II, the status and the functions of the deacon are being reconsidered. The issue is made peculiarly urgent by the state of that Church in Latin America. There, where the overwhelming majority of the population is at least nominally Catholic and where a dearth of priests, both in numbers and quality, is chronic, can deacons, possibly married, assist in ministering to the rank and file of the Catholics through functions such as catechetical instruction, which canonically are permissible to deacons?

Another variety of the diaconate has been the office of deaconess. We hear of them in the early Church, and they figured prominently in the eastern wing of the Catholic Church. As a specific office, that of deaconess was not outstanding in

Western Europe in the Middle Ages. In the nineteenth century they were revived in the Anglican communion and in Lutheranism and some other Protestant churches.

From this brief summary of what has been presented in the preceding chapters, it must be obvious that, in its many variations from the earliest days, the diaconate has been a feature of the Church. Again and again it has been formalized. Often it has seemed to have become vestigial, preserved because it was one of the historical offices of the Church, but it has survived and has been revived repeatedly. Today it is vigorous. Never before has it displayed so many forms. Here is vitality.

Two questions are inescapable. Is the diaconate essential or is it simply useful? Is it of the *esse* or the *bene esse* of the Church as conceived by Christ? If it is of the *esse* of the Church, what should be its purpose and its functions?

Again and again we have recorded sayings of our Lord which seem to indicate that the diaconate is of the *esse* of the Church. The preceding chapters have consistently reminded us that the English word "deacon" is an Anglicanized form of a Greek word which appears repeatedly in the New Testament. It is the Greek equivalent of the Aramaic term by which Jesus characterized his central purpose, and which he said should be reflected in his disciples. "Whosoever will be great among you shall be your minister (*diakonos*); and whoever of you will be the chiefest shall be servant (*doulos*) of all. For even the Son of Man came not to be ministered unto (*diakonesthenai*) but to minister (*diakonesai*) and to give his life as a ransom for many" (Mk 10,43-45, and its parallel, Mt 10,26-28).

So, too, in the early Church, in enumerating the gifts of Christ to "the saints in Ephesus," the letter to them speaks (Eph 4,9-12) of apostles, prophets, evangelists, pastors, and teachers, and as all of them being "for the perfecting of the saints, for the work of ministry (*diakonias*)," seeming to imply that all members of the Church shared in *diakonia* or the diaconate. Therefore, *diakonia* is of the *esse* of the Church.

Sometimes the New Testament speaks of *diakonia* as ministry to physical needs. Thus, after her healing by Christ, Peter's wife's mother "ministered" (*diekonei*) to those about her (Mk 1,21). The term was applied also to the women who accompanied Christ and the twelve and who ministered (*diekonoun*) of their substance (Lk 8,1-3). So Paul speaks of the gifts he was collecting from Gentile Churches for the distressed Christians in Jerusalem as ministering (*diakonias*) to the saints (2 Cor 8,4, 9,1). The widows in the Jerusalem Church were ministered to (*diakonia*) daily, and it was to ensure that in this there was no discrimination that the seven were appointed (Acts 6,1-6). We must hasten to point out that the seven were not necessarily the first deacons, and that the New Testament does not limit *diakonia* to ministering to physical needs. Nor does the New Testament use of the word in its several forms exclude the variety of functions which we have noted as characterizing the diaconate in the long history of the Church.

Since *diakonia* in one or another of its expressions is of the *esse* of the Church, what of the diaconate? Is it too of the *esse*, or is it of the *bene esse* of the Church, useful but dispensable? If by the diaconate is meant an office bearing that name, clearly it is not indispensable. For example, the Society of Friends does not have an institution by that title, yet its record has been and continues to be one of distinguished *diakonia*—of that the American Friends Service Committee is ample evidence. By its name "service" and its history it is practicing *diakonia*, but none of its officers or staff has the official title "deacon." So, too, the World Council of Churches, while stressing *diakonia* in its various forms of meeting physical needs, does not operate through representatives who are officially designated "deacons."

Yet obviously the office or institution of the diaconate is characteristic of the Churches which embrace the overwhelming majority of those who are called Christians, and seems destined to persist indefinitely. That is not because of "social lag"—perpetuation through inertia, or out of respect for history. That may be true of some branches of the Church; but the diaconate continues to have useful functions, so vital to the life of the Church that, if it did not exist, they would have to be assigned to some office especially created for that purpose. That is seen in the majority of Protestant Churches. In many of them the deacons share in administering Holy Communion. Theoretically, and often actually, they assist the pastor in the "cure of souls"—ministering to the spiritual welfare of the members of the Church. In some Churches they are ordained. In one way or another, usually informally, they are often given specific training for the fulfillment of their functions. One of the preceding chapters has described the permanent diaconate in one diocese in the Episcopal Church. Presumably, it similarly exists in other branches of the Anglican communion. An informative chapter describes the manner in which Vatican II took significant action in modifying and strengthening the diaconate. Although the New Testament teaches that every Christian should share in *diakonia,* it also gives examples of assigning responsibility for some phases of that mission. Lately we have been hearing, and rightly so, that "the Church is mission," but that mission, as the New Testament and the experience of all the subsequent centuries makes obvious, can best be effected through a variety of offices. Of these the diaconate is one. So far as the historian can see, the diaconate will be continued and will assist the Church in fulfilling the purpose which the Lord of the Church has for it.

NOTES

Deacons in History and Practice

1. I owe this phrase to the Very Rev. Damasus Winzen, O.S.B., now Prior of St. Saviour's Monastery, Elmira, New York.

2. Lucian, *Alexander the False Prophet*, 5.

3. See discussion of this passage by A. M. Farrer, "The Ministry in the New Testament," in K. E. Kirk, *The Apostolic Ministry* (1946), pp. 147–148.

4. In Migne, *Patrologia Graeca*, Vol. XXXVII, cols. 389–395.

5. The so-called *Apostolic Church Order*, probably East Syrian about A. D. 200.

6. For text translated above, see Gregory Dix, ed., *The Treatise on the Apostolic Tradition of St. Hippolytus of Rome* (London, 1937), pp. 17–18.

7. R. Hugh Connolly, ed., *Didascalia Apostolorum* (Oxford, 1929), Chapter IX, pp. 86–88.

8. *Ibid.*, Chapter XVI, pp. 146–151.

9. *Ibid.*, Chapter XI, p. 117, Chapter XII, pp. 120–123.

10. Eusebius, *Church History*, VI, 43, 11; Cornelius probably wrote *in ecclesia catholica*, meaning in the orthodox church at Rome as distinguished from heresies and schisms.

11. *Acta Cypriani* 5; for the proceedings at Cirta, see Optatus of Mileve, *Against the Donatists*, Appendix (*Gesta apud Zenophilum*).

12. Cyprian, Letter 80 (81); Roman Breviary, first antiphon of Matins (August 10); the legend of death on a gridiron derives from rhetorical language about the fiery trial of martyrdom.

13. For the Canons of Arles, see conveniently J. Stevenson, *A New*

Eusebius (London, 1957), pp. 321–325; the Eastern canons which will be quoted are translated in Henry Percival, *The Seven Ecumenical Councils* (*Nicene and Post-Nicene Fathers*, Series II, Vol. XIV), (New York, 1900).

14. See T. G. Jalland, "The Doctrine of the Parity of Ministers," in Kirk, *The Apostolic Ministry*, pp. 314–316; a possible case is the deacon Sanctus who seems in 177 to have been the only cleric of Vienne (Letter of the Martyrs of Lyons in Eusebius, *Church History*, V, 1, 17); about 304 the Council of Elvira refers to the deacon in charge of a congregation (*diaconus regens plebem*) as sometimes happens in the Episcopal Church today—candidates whom he baptizes must be confirmed by the bishop (can. 77).

15. The author was, perhaps, Pope Damasus' opponent, Isaac the Jew. Alexander Souter, ed., *Pseudo-Augustini Quaestiones Veteris et Novi Testamenti* (Vienna, 1908), CSEL 50, 193–198.

16. See E. G. Cuthbert F. Atchley, ed., *Ordo Romanus Primus* (London, 1905), Introduction, pp. 28–30; present usage in Missal of John XXIII (1960), *Rubricae Generales*, No. 137, *Planetae plicatae et stola latior amplius non adhibentur*; earlier in *Caeremoniale Episcoporum* (Rome, 1600), Bk. II, 14, 9.

17. Present customs first appear clearly in the liturgy of the *Apostolic Constitutions*, Bk. VIII, representing Syrian usage of about 375; and at Jerusalem in the Pilgrimage of Etheria a few years later; for Theodore of Mopsuestia, see his *Commentary on the Lord's Prayer and on the Sacraments of Baptism and the Eucharist* (Woodbrooke Studies [Cambridge, 1933], Vol. VI, 95 ff.).

18. For the rather complex customs of the eighth century, see *Ordo Romanus Primus*, pp. 14–15, 19–20; for Gregory's change, see Canon 1 of the Roman Council of 595.

19. Leo, Letters 113, 117, 132; Gregory, *Register*, I, 19, 20; II, 18, 19 (quoted above); III, 32.

20. Liberatus, *Breviarium Causarum Nestorianorum et Eutychianorum*, pp. 21, 23; Procopius, *Secret History*, pp. 27, 17.

21. Procopius, *Wars*, VII, 16; XX, 23–24; XXI, 17–18.

22. The appropriately named subdeacon, Servusdei, served as his messenger (see Percival, *op. cit.*, p. 304).

23. Gregory, as *septimus diaconus* in the *Life* by John the Deacon, I, 25; his deacon, Honoratus, at Constantinople, in *Register*, I, 6, 49; Peter, subdeacon of Sicily, later of Campania, in *Register*, III, 1, and frequently.

24. See Atchley, *Ordo Romanus Primus*, Introduction, pp. 34–36.

25. Louis Delatte, *Commentary on the Rule of St. Benedict*, tr., Justin McCann (London, 1921), p. 525, quoting Luc d'Achery, *Spicilegium*, Vol. IV, p. 229; in 1964, a modern Russian Orthodox mon-

astery, Holy Trinity, Jordanville, New York, had in its community a bishop, fifteen priests, and four deacons: *Parishes and Clergy of the Orthodox and Other Eastern Churches* (Buffalo, 1964), p. 93.

26. For details of the older rites, see Pierre DePuniet, *The Roman Pontifical*, tr., Justin McCann (London, 1932), pp. 170–215.

27. January 8–February 22: Michael Wilks, *The Problem of Sovereignty in the Later Middle Ages* (Cambridge, 1963), p. 389; for other cases, see M. Wilks, "The Apostolicus and the Bishop of Rome," in *Journal of Theological Studies*, N. S. (1963), Vol. XIV, 325–326.

28. *Reformatio ecclesiarum Hassiae*, Chapters 3 and 24–25 in B. J. Kidd, ed., *Documents Illustrative of the Continental Reformation* (Oxford, 1911), pp. 225, 230.

29. T. A. Lacey, ed., *The King's Book, or a Necessary Doctrine and Erudition for Any Christian Man, 1543* (London, 1932), pp. 68–69.

30. Quoted in Philip Caraman, ed., *The Other Face, Catholic Life under Elizabeth I* (New York, 1960), p. 268.

31. John Strype, *Annals of the Reformation and Establishment of Religion and Other Various Occurrences in the Church of England during Queen Elizabeth's Happy Reign*, new ed. (Oxford, 1824), II, part II, p. 170.

32. Richard Hooker, *Laws of Ecclesiastical Polity*, Bk. V, 78, 5; the *Admonition* and Whitgift are quoted in the footnotes on this passage in the edition by John Keble, 6th ed. (London, 1874), II, pp. 474–475.

33. When he was ordained with Philip Muhlenberg and another candidate who had been made deacons a few days before: W. S. Perry, "Ancestry and Early Life," in W. H. Stowe, ed., *The Life and Letters of Bishop White* (New York, 1937), pp. 26–32.

34. John Beresford, ed., *The Diary of a Country Parson*, 5 vols. (Oxford, 1926–1931), I, p. 26.

35. R. D. Middleton, *Dr. Routh* (Oxford, 1938), pp. 40, 191–196. A more recent permanent diaconate at Oxford was that of Charles Plummer, editor of Bede and chaplain of Corpus Christi College.

36. See discussion of Canon 35 in E. A. White and Jackson A. Dykman, *Annotated Constitution and Canons for the Government of the Protestant Episcopal Church in the United States of America*, 2 vols. (Greenwich, 1954), I, pp. 593–612.

37. The collect for a layman was said with addition of the title, "thy servant N., Cardinal Deacon."

38. See regulations of 1939–40 in *Acts of the Convocations of Canterbury and York* (London, 1961), pp. 53–61.

39. See comments of various writers in Alonzo Potter, ed., *Memorial Papers* (Philadelphia, 1857).

40. Most recently in 1961, when the clerical order also defeated the proposal (*Journal of the General Convention of the Protestant Episcopal Church, 1961*, p. 199). (It was adopted in 1967.)

41. In Isabel Hapgood, tr., *Service Book of the Holy Orthodox-Catholic Apostolic Church* (New York, 1922), p. 313.

The Deacon in Protestantism

1. The petition is given by Albert Peel, *The First Congregational Churches* (Cambridge, 1920), p. 33. See also pp. 36, 46.

2. The First Admonition to Parliament in R. E. Prothero, *Statutes and Constitutional Documents 1558–1625*, 4th ed., (Oxford, 1913), p. 199.

3. Compare the following statements:

"The Apostles and Ministers at first did not bynde them selves to anye one order in theire proceedinges and governement; it is not like, that ever they meant to bynde the Churche of god to anye one." Thus Bancroft, writing against the rigid views of the Separatists and Puritans, *Tracts ascribed to Richard Bancroft*, ed., Albert Peel (Cambridge, 1953), p. 107.

"Between a form of church government and those great truths concerning Christ and the Christian redemption which form the chief part of the substance of the New Testament there is an obvious difference. What is true once is true for ever. . . . But a form of church government which was the best possible organisation for the Church in the first century may, perhaps, have been the worst possible organisation for the Church in the third." Robert Dale so writes in defending Congregationalism in the nineteenth century against high church Anglicanism, *Congregational Principles* (1920 ed.), p. 4 f.

4. See John Wesley's comments upon church polity in his *Journal* for January 20th, 1746.

5. "The Babylonish Captivity of the Church," in *Luther's Primary Works*, ed., Henry Wace and C. A. Buchheim (London, 1896), p. 400.

6. See *Evangelisches Kirchenlexicon*, ed., Heinz Brunotte and Otto Weber (Gottingen, 1956 ff.), I, 915 f.; articles on "Diakon," "Diakonie."

7. "The Nature of the Ministry," *Monday Morning*, Aug. 1964 (Philadelphia), p. 24.

8. This was my view when I wrote this chapter, but recently I have had to modify it on reading Manfred Kurt Bahmann, "The Development of Luther's Principle of Ecclesiastical Authority (1512–1530) in the German Reformation." (Unpublished Ph.D. thesis, The Hartford Seminary Foundation, 1967.) Dr. Bahmann convinces me that in the provisions

Luther made for the Leisnig congregation, and in his treatise *On the Ministry* prepared for the Bohemians, Luther had developed a very clear ecclesiology during the early years of the Reformation that reflected many of the features of later New Testament "Restorationism." But Bahmann also shows very convincingly that 1) Luther avoided the Restorationist trap by basing his ecclesiology upon biblical *theology* rather than upon biblical literalism. This enabled him to attempt ·a reconciliation between the "gathered church" and the "parish church" concepts. 2) The experiment failed largely because people were not ready for it, and the practical problems that arose in 1524–25 forced Luther more and more to rely upon temporary expedients based upon the relatively stable authority of the local rulers in order to guarantee the ongoing life of the evangelical churches. The later ecclesiastical settlements of Lutheranism reflect these *ad hoc* arrangements rather than Luther's basic ecclesiology.

9. E.g., the *Savoy Declaration* (see n. 11) of 1658 does little to define the office.

10. *An Apologeticall Narration*, ed., Robert S. Paul, facsimile edition (Philadelphia and Boston, 1963), p. 8.

11. *The Savoy Declaration of Faith and Order 1658*, ed., A. G. Matthews (London, 1959), Art. XI on Polity, p. 123.

12. H. Wheeler Robinson, *The Life and Faith of the Baptists* (London, n.d.), p. 8 f.

13. Royal J. Montgomery, *A Manual for Deacons and Deaconesses of the Congregational Christian Churches* (Boston and Chicago, n.d.), p. 3. The manual goes on to say that "some denominations have emphasized the functions of oversight and management, and call these leaders 'elders.' Congregational and other Christian churches have emphasized the fraternal and service activities. 'Elders govern, deacons serve'" (p. 4). Apart from a criticism of 'elders' which is somewhat less than generous, this statement seems to be curiously blind to Congregational history. Nowhere did the Ruling Elder have more authority than in the Congregational churches of New England. In any case, ought one to speak of an elder's "governing," or about his spiritual authority?

14. *Ibid.*, p. 3. In British Congregational churches, no distinction is made between deacons and deaconesses; they are members of a single order.

15. Harold Bickley, *The High Calling and Work of a Deacon* (London, n.d.), p. 8 f.

16. William Barnett Blakemore, "The Christian Task and the Church's Ministry," *The Revival of the Churches*, ed., W. B. Blakemore (St. Louis, 1963), III, 153, 154.

17. Jeremiah Burroughes, *Irenicum, to the Lovers of Truth and Peace* (London, 1646), p. 51.

18. I have taken a tentative step in this direction in my book, *Ministry* (Grand Rapids, Michigan, 1965).

19. B. H. Streeter, *The Primitive Church* (New York and London, 1929), p. ix.

20. *The Revival of the Churches*, p. 52 f.

21. Arnold Ehrhardt, *The Apostolic Succession* (London, 1953). See, by the same author, *The Apostolic Ministry* (Edinburgh, 1958).

22. This is part of the thesis in my book, *Ministry*.

23. "A Booke which sheweth the life and manners of all true Christians" (Middleburgh, 1582), Section 54, in *The Writings of Robert Harrison and Robert Browne*, ed. Albert Peel and Leland H. Carlson (London, 1953), p. 275.

24. "Of Deacons," in the *Form of Government, The Constitution of the United Presbyterian Church in the United States of America 1964–65*, p. 124.

25. Dwight E. Stevenson, in the Disciples' publication, *The Revival of the Churches*, suggests that "the Seven" in Acts 6 were not deacons; *op. cit.*, p. 40.

26. This does not mean that there were no examples of evangelism— John Eliot's work among the Indians was notable in this respect. But it appears that the Congregational Puritans of New England regarded the pastor as an evangelist, and it became a point at issue between them and the Reformed churches of continental Europe. See John Norton, *The Answer*, ed. and trans., Douglas Horton (Cambridge, Mass., 1958), ch. 8, p. 108 ff.

27. W. W. Sweet, *The Story of Religion in America* (New York, 1939), p. 314.

28. *The Nature of the Ministry*, (above, note 7), p. 35.

29. *Ibid.*, ch. V, "Of Deacons," pp. 24 ff.

The Order of Diaconate in the Roman Catholic Church

1. "Die Theologie der Erneuerung des Diakonates" (The Theology of a Revival of the Diaconate) in *Diaconia in Christo: über die Erneuerung des Diakonates*," ed., Karl Rahner and Herbert Vorgrimler (Freiburg, 1962). See *Quaestiones disputatae* (New York, 1965), Vol. 15/16, pp. 285 ff.

2. Heinrich Flatten, "Der Diakon nach dem heutigen Recht der lateinischen Kirche" (The Deacon in the Present-day Law of the Latin Church) in *"Diaconia . . . ,"* p. 129 ff.

3. Herbert Krimm, "Das Diakonat in der frühkatholischen Kirche"

(The Diaconate in the Early Catholic Church) in *Das diakonische Amt der Kirche* (The Diaconal Office of the Church), ed., Dr. Herbert Krimm (Stuttgart, 1953).

4. Walter Croce, "Die Niederen Weihen und ihre hierarchische Wertung" (The Minor Orders and their Place in the Hierarchy) in *Zeitschrift für Katholische Theologie* (Vienna, 1948), Vol. 3, esp. Chapter IV, "Der Reformversuch des Tridentinischen Konzils" (The Attempted Reform of the Council of Trent), 307 ff. See also Paul Winninger, *Vers un renouveau du diaconat* (Paris, 1958), p. 181 ff.

5. *Acts of the Council of Trent*, edited by the Görres-Gesellschaft (Freiburg, 1901–), Vol. 9, ed., Stephan Ehses, 592 ff.

6. "Epistolae P. Hieronymi Nadal, S. J.," in *Monumenta Historica Societatis Jesu* (Madrid, 1902), III, 343 ff.

7. J. Hornef, "Vom Werden und Wachsen des Anliegens" (The Origin and Development of the Diaconate Movement) in *Diaconia* . . . , p. 343 ff.

8. J. Hornef, *The New Vocation* (Cork, 1963, German ed., Vienna, 1959); see also Winninger, as in note 4, and Schamoni, as quoted in text; also J. Paulo Nunes, *A hora do diacono* (Lisbon, 1961), and Manuel Useros Carretero, *Nuevos diaconos?* (Barcelona, 1962). Most important is the work given in footnote 1.

9. *Diaconia* . . . , p. 412 ff.

10. J. Hornef, "Die Frage der Erneuerung des Diakonats vor dem Konzil" (The Question of the Revival of the Diaconate before the Council) in *Deutsche Tagespost*, Nos. 37 and 38, 1964.

11. J. Hornef, "Brauchen wir auch den jungen hauptberuflichen Diakon?" (Do We also Need the Young Full-time Deacon?), in *Caritas* (Lucerne, 8/9, 1963).

12. W. Abbott, S.J., *The Documents of Vatican II* (New York, 1966), pp. 55–56.

13. Bishop Frotz, "Pastoralblatt für die Diözesen Aachen" (Essen und Köln, 1964), No. 12, p. 357.

The Problem of Diaconate in the Orthodox Church

1. See the comments on the Trullan Canon by Zonaras, Balsamon and Aristenos, in the *Syntagma*, ed., G. A. Ralle and M. Potle (Athens, 1852), II, 340–343.

2. As, for instance, by the late Professor Nicholas Gloubokovsky, the renowned student of New Testament and Patristics, and by the late Professor Alexander Almazov, a distinguished canonist and liturgiologist.

See their statements in *Zhournaly and Protokoly Predsobornago Pri-sutstvija* (Diaries and Minutes of the Pre-Council Commission) (St. Petersburg, 1907), III, 220, 223.

3. *The Treatise on the Apostolic Tradition of St. Hippolytus of Rome*, ed., Gregory Dix (London, 1937), pp. 15–18; Jean Michel Hanssens, S.J., *La Liturgie d'Hippolyte* (Orientalia Christiana Analecta, 155), (Rome, 1959), p. 122 f., 166 f., 401 ff.; Dom Bernard Botte, O.S.B., *La Tradition Apostolique de Saint Hippolyte, Essai de Reconstruction* (Liturgiegeschichtliche Quellen und Forschungen (Munster/W.), Hf. 39, p. 23 ff. and *passim*; Jean Colson, *La fonction diaconale aux origines de l'Eglise* (1960), pp. 97–104.

4. For instance, Anton Baumstark, *Die Messe im Morgenland* (Kempten und Munich, 1906), p. 12 ff.; "Vom geschichtlichen Werden der Liturgie," in *Ecclesia Orans*, 10 (Freiburg i/Br., 1923) pp. 97 ff.

5. The relevant texts are collected and examined in the recent book by S. Salaville and G. Nowack, *Le rôle du diacre dans la Liturgie Orientale* (Paris-Athens, 1962, 'Archives de l'Orient Chrétien,' 3), pp. 34–43.

6. By Baumstark, as quoted above in Note 4; by Salaville and Nowack, *op. cit.*, Note 5, pp. 117–119; also by I. H. Dalmais, O.P., *Le Diacre, guide de la prière du peuple d'après la tradition liturgique*, in *La Maison-Dieu*, 61, 1960, pp. 30–40.

7. I. M. Hanssens, *Institutiones liturgicae de ritibus orientalibus* (Rome, 1932), III, p. 230.

8. Nicholas Cabasilas, *Sacrae liturgiae interpretatio*, c. XII and XIV, *MG CL*, c. 393, 397.

9. *Ibid.*, c. XV, c. 399, 401.

10. This was the hypothesis of Père Dalmais, *op. cit.*, Note 6, p. 37. Baumstark did not think so: *Die Messe in Morgenland*, p. 12.

11. Baumstark, *Vom geschichtlichen Werden . . .* , p. 97 ff.

12. See my article, "Corpus Mysticum: The Eucharist and Catholicity, in *Church Service Society Annual*, No. 9, May 1936–1937 (Cupar, Scotland), pp. 38–46.

13. For further information: A. Goloubtsov, "O prichinakh i vremeni zameny glasnago chtenija liturgijnykh molitv tapnym" (On the Causes and the Time of the Change of the Audible Recitation of Liturgical Prayers into the Secret), in *Bogoslovskij Vestnik* (September, 1905), pp. 69–75; B. Sove, "Eucharistija v drevnej Tserkvi i sovremennaja praktika" (The Eucharist in the Ancient Church and the Contemporary Practice), *Zhivoje Predanie* (Paris, n.d.), pp. 179 ff.; Panagiotis Trembelas, "L'Audition de l'Anaphora Eucharistique par le Peuple," *L'Eglise et les Eglises*, II, Editions de Chevetogne (Belgium, 1955), 207–220; see also the remarks of Archimandrite Kiprian (Kern), *Eucharistija* (Paris, 1947), p. 165 ff.

14. See, for instance, the intervention of Archbishop Dimitry (Kovalnicky) of Kherson and Odessa at the Pre-Conciliar Consultation in 1906 in *Zhournaly i Protokoly*, as quoted above, Note 2, III, 223 f. Archbishop Dimitry was previously for about thirty years Professor of Ecclesiastical History in the Theological Academy of Kiev, and later its rector. Subsequently he served as bishop of Tambov, archbishop of Kazan, and finally of Kherson and Odessa, and was an influential member of the holy governing Synod of the Russian Church (d. 1913).

15. See the remarks of Father Kiprian, *op. cit.*, pp. 137 ff.

16. For further information see the competent book of A. V. Preobrazhensky, *Kultovaja Musyka v Rossii* (The Cult Music in Russia), (Leningrad, 1924). Preobrazhensky was the Director of the School of Sacred Music (Pridvornaja Pevcheskaja Kapella) in St. Petersburg before the Revolution. See also the recent articles of Johann von Gardner, "Drei Typen des Russischen Kirchengesangs" and "Stilistische Ruchtungen im Russischen liturgischen Chorgesang," *Ostkirchliche Studien* (Wurzburg, Bd. VI, 4, 1951 and Bd. XI, 2/3, 1962).

17. See my article, "The Sacrament of Pentecost," *Journal of the Fellowship of St. Alban and St. Sergius*, No. 23 (London, 1934).

18. See the interesting attempt of Joseph Lecuyer, C.S.Sp., to formulate the principles of a "spirituality of the diaconate," in *Dictionnaire de Spiritualité*, fasc. XX–XXI (Paris, 1955), s.v. "Diaconat," p. 810 ff. It is based mainly on the analysis of the scriptural texts.

19. There is no up-to-date monograph on the history of the Russian clergy. Some information is given in general manuals of Church history, especially in that of Professor A. Dobroklonsky, Vol. IV, published in the last decade of the last century. One has still reference to old books of Professor Peter Znamensky: *Prikhodskoe Dukhovenstvo v Rossii so vremeni reform Petra* (The Parish Clergy in Russia since the Time of Peter's Reforms), (Kazan, 1873), and *Dukhovnyja Shkoly v Rossii de reformy 1808 goda* (The Church Schools in Russia up to the Reform of 1808), (Kazan, 1881). See also N. Runovsky, *Tserkovnograzhdanskie zakonopolozhenija otnositel'no pravoslavnago dukhovenstva v tsarstvovanie Imp. Alexandra II* (The Church and State Legislation Concerning the Orthodox Clergy in the Reign of Alexander II), (Kazan, 1898).

20. See Sergius Troitsky, *Diakonissy v Pravoslavnoj Tserkvi* (The Deaconess in the Orthodox Church), (St. Petersburg, 1912).

The Order of Deacons in Anglicanism

1. M. H. Shepherd, Jr., *The Oxford American Prayer Book Commentary* (New York, 1950), p. 532 f.

2. *The Book of Common Prayer,* p. 533. (See Chapter I, p. 28 above for 1550 version.)

3. W. Pell and P. M. Dawley, *The Religion of the Prayer Book* (New York, 1950), p. 200.

4. See Canon 34, *Constitution and Canons for the Government of the Protestant Episcopal Church in the United States of America.* (See 1967 General Convention's edition for most recent changes.)

5. Canon Law provides for the shortening of the year to six months, a practice regulated at diocesan levels (Canon 35, Sec. 2).

6. W. Pell and P. M. Dawley, *op. cit.,* p. 201.

7. Normally the preparation for the ministry in the American Church includes a bachelor's degree from a college offering at least basic studies in the liberal arts and sciences, plus three years of seminary education leading to either a degree of Bachelor of Divinity or of Sacred Theology. In addition, the examinations listed in Canon Law are administered at diocesan levels. For the perpetual diaconate, however, there are a variety of less structured methods of preparation and canonical examinations of less magnitude (Canon 34, Sec. 10).

8. At this point the clause discussed in this essay's subsequent paragraph was included.

9. Canon 34, Section 10 C; prior to 1964 edition.

10. *Ibid.,* 1964 edition.

11. *The Book of Common Prayer,* p. 535.

12. Additional pertinent information can be found in the following studies: H. Boone Porter, "The Ministers of the Distribution of Holy Communion" (Supplemental Report II prepared for the Standing Liturgical Commission of the Episcopal Church in the United States of America, 1964), available through the Executive Council of the Episcopal Church, New York; and, "A Self-Supporting Ministry and the Mission of the Church" (a report published by the Division of Christian Ministries of the Executive Council of the Episcopal Church and the Overseas Mission Society, 1964), including relevant bibliographical data.

13. Nicolas Stacey, "A Mission's Failure," in *The London Observer* (Sunday Supplement), December 6, 1954, p. 33.

14. Philip A. Anderson, "The Implication and Challenge of O. Hobart Mowrer's Position for the Church and its Ministry," in *The Minister's Quarterly,* XX, No. 2 (Summer, 1964), 2.

15. Justus G. Lawler, "The Problem of Priests in the World," *Commonweal,* April 16, 1965, 106.

16. *Ibid.,* p. 107.

17. Harvey Cox, *The Secular City* (New York, 1965), p. 246.

The Office of Deaconess

1. The Vulgate reads: *"in ministerio ecclesiae."*

2. Joseph B. Lightfoot, *On A Fresh Revision of the English New Testament* (New York, 1871), p. 114.

3. J. S. Howson, *The Diaconate of Women in the Anglican Church* (London, 1886), p. 33.

4. Pliny's Letter to Trajan, *Ep. lib.* x., xcvi, quoted in *The Ministry of Women: A Report by a Committee Appointed by His Grace The Lord Archbishop of Canterbury* (London and New York, 1919), p. 5.

5. William Collins, "On the Early History and Modern Revival of Deaconesses," in *The Ministry of Women*, p. 112.

6. *Loc cit.*

7. See J. A. Robinson's contribution, Appendix A, in Cecilia Robinson, *The Ministry of Deaconesses* (London, 1898), p. 200.

8. *Ibid.*, p. 210 f.

9. *The Ministry of Women*, p. 7 f.; p. 11.

10. *Ibid.*, p. 59.

11. See J. A. Robinson, Appendix C, in Cecilia Robinson, *op. cit.*, pp. 233 f.

12. *Loc. cit.*

13. J. M. Ludlow, *Woman's Work in the Church* (New York, 1866), p. 28.

14. Cecilia Robinson, *op. cit.*, Ch. 2 and 3.

15. J. M. Ludlow, *op. cit.*, p. 51 ff. and Cecilia Robinson, *op. cit.*, p. 76 ff.

16. See J. A. Robinson, Appendix A, *op. cit.*, pp. 209 ff.

17. See J. A. Robinson, Appendix B, *op. cit.*, p. 220.

18. L. A. Muratori, *Antiquities of Italy* (Milan, 1741), V, 577.

19. See J. A. Robinson, Appendix B., *op. cit.*, p. 228.

20. *The Ministry of Women*, p. 11.

21. Joseph Bingham, *The Antiquities of the Christian Church* (London, 1867), Book III, Chapter 1, p. 107.

22. William Collins, *op. cit.*, p. 117.

23. *The Ministry of Women*, pp. 60, 121.

24. Cecilia Robinson, *op. cit.*, p. 60.

25. *Ibid.*, p. 88.

26. William Collins, *op. cit.*, p. 122 (footnote 8).

27. Cecilia Robinson, *op. cit.*, p. 89.

28. William Collins, *op. cit.*, p. 125 f. for charters.

29. See J. A. Robinson, Appendix B, *op. cit.*, p. 228.

30. *Ibid.*, p. 229.

31. Cecilia Robinson, *op. cit.*, p. 99.

32. *The Ministry of Women*, p. 9.

33. See William Collins, *op. cit.*, p. 129.

34. Alban Butler, *Lives of the Saints*, rev. D. Attwater (New York, 1956), Vol. III, p. 143.

35. *The Ministry of Women*, p. 278 ff.

36. See Henry C. Potter, *Sisterhood and Deaconesses* (New York, 1873) for partial list of these experiments.

37. Walter C. Whitaker, *History of the Protestant Episcopal Church in Alabama: 1763–1891* (Birmingham, 1898), p. 144 ff.

38. Richard H. Wilmer, "Form of Service for Institution of Deaconesses in the Diocese of Alabama" (Birmingham, 1885), p. 9.

39. William Collins, *op. cit.*, p. 125 or footnote 5.

40. *The Ministry of Women*, p. 214.

41. Walter C. Whitaker, *op. cit.*

42. *The Ministry of Women*, etc.

43. The *Reports* of the Lambeth Conference are published after each Conference by S.P.C.K.; see the Reports of 1930 and 1948.

44. See Canon 50, *Constitution and Canons for the Government of the Protestant Episcopal Church in the United States of America* (New York, 1967).

45. From Canon 20, prior to the revision of 1922; see *Journals* of General Convention (New York, triennially after General Convention).

46. Canon 50, 1964 and subsequent edition.

47. Joseph B. Lightfoot, *op. cit.*, p. 114; Cecelia Robinson, *op. cit.*, p. 15.

LIST OF CONTRIBUTORS

EDMOND LaB. CHERBONNIER, chairman of the religion department at Trinity College, Hartford, Conn., earned degrees at Harvard University, Union Theological Seminary, Cambridge University, and Columbia University. Prior to assuming his present position, he taught at Union Theological Seminary, Vassar College, and Barnard College of Columbia University and was Deacon at the Cathedral Church of St. John the Divine, New York. The author of *Hardness of Heart*, Dr. Cherbonnier has contributed articles to a number of scholarly journals.

GEORGE H. EMERSON is Archdeacon of the Episcopal Diocese of California and Chancellor of St. Andrew's Parish, Saratoga, California. A lawyer by training, Archdeacon Emerson was ordained a deacon in 1960 and has been active in parish and diocesan affairs.

THEODORE PARKER FERRIS, Rector of Trinity Church, Boston, Mass. since 1942, was educated at Harvard University, Union Theological Seminary, and General Theological Seminary, New

York. A noted preacher and pastor, Dr. Ferris has authored a number of books, including *Go Tell the People*, and contributed to *The Interpreter's Bible*.

GEORGES FLOROVSKY is visiting professor of history and religion at Princeton University, New Jersey, and professor of Eastern Church history, emeritus, at Harvard University. He was educated at the University of Odessa and the Russian University Center, Prague, and is the recipient of honorary degrees. A member of the Faith and Order Commission of the World Council of Churches, he is the author of *Eastern Fathers of the Fourth Century, Byzantine Fathers of the Fifth Through the Eighth Centuries, Ways of Russian Theology*, and numerous scholarly articles.

EDWARD R. HARDY, professor of church history at Berkeley Divinity School, New Haven, Conn., since 1947, was educated at Columbia University, General Theological Seminary, and Union Theological Seminary, New York. He has been a participant in theological discussions at the World Council of Churches, and among his scholarly publications are *Militant in Earth: Twenty Centuries of the Spread of Christianity* and (ed.) *Christology of the Later Fathers* in the "Library of Christian Classics."

JOSEF HORNEF was for many years District Court Judge in Fulda, Germany, and holds the degree of *Doctor utriusque juris*. The author of numerous scholarly articles about the restoration of the diaconate in the Roman Catholic Church, as well as the role of the layman, Dr. Hornef is the author of the book *Kommt der Diakon der frühen Kirche wieder?* which has been published in English as *The New Vocation*. Dr. Hornef resides today in Fulda.

KENNETH SCOTT LATOURETTE is Sterling Professor of Missions and Oriental History, Emeritus, at Yale University. Educated at Linfield College, Oregon, and Yale University, Dr. Latourette has been awarded numerous honorary degrees. "Recognized and established as the pre-eminent Protestant historian of the twentieth century" (*The Christian Herald*), his works include the seven-volume *History of the Expansion of Christianity, A History of Christianity,* and *Christianity Through the Ages.*

ARNOLD H. LEGG was educated at Cambridge University and Fitzwilliam Hall and Cheshunt Theological College. He served as a Congregational minister in the South India United Church and later as a bishop in the Church of South India at its inception in 1947 until his retirement in 1966. His final post was as Moderator of the Church of South India (1962-1966), and in this capacity was an Observer at the recent Vatican Council. Bishop Legg, now residing in England, contributed the chapter "Bishops in the Church of South India" in the volume *Bishops* (London, 1961) and is the author of *Christian Baptism: Its Practice and Its Meaning.*

RICHARD T. NOLAN is instructor in philosophy and education at Hartford Seminary Foundation (for 1967-8) and lecturer in philosophy at the Universities of Connecticut and Hartford; since 1965 he has been an associate minister at Trinity Church Parish, Bristol, Connecticut. Educated at Trinity College (Conn.), Berkeley Divinity School, Hartford Seminary Foundation, Yale University and New York University, Mr. Nolan taught formerly at Watkinson School, Cathedral School of the Cathedral Church of St. John the Divine, and the Cheshire Academy.

ROBERT S. PAUL is professor of modern church history at the Pittsburgh Theological Seminary, Pennsylvania, a post which he assumed in the fall of 1967. Educated at Oxford University, he has held parish posts, attended the first assembly of the World Council of Churches, and was Associate Director of the Graduate School of Ecumenical Studies in Switzerland. From

1958 to 1967 Dr. Paul was Waldo Professor of Church History at Hartford Seminary Foundation. He is the author of *The Lord Protector*, a biography of Oliver Cromwell, *The Atonement and the Sacraments, Ministry,* and several scholarly essays, including contributions to the Encyclopaedia Britannica and *Weltkirchenlexicon.*

PATRICK RUSSELL is a curate in the rural area of Hollyford, Ireland, where he is a member of the (Roman Catholic) Cashel Diocesan Priests Council. Educated at University College, Ireland, and Yale University, where he specialized in German literature, Father Russell is a veteran translator for Dr. Hornef.

MARY P. TRUESDELL was ordered deaconess in 1919 and has served in a number of parishes of the Episcopal Church. Educated at Milwaukee-Downer College and the Philadelphia training center for deaconesses, she is the author of *The Deaconess Office and Ministry* and *Does the Church Want Deaconesses?*